I0149559

CAN I SIT WITH YOU?

The Stormy Social Seas of the Schoolyard

SHANNON DES ROCHES ROSA and JENNIFER BYDE MYERS

Deadwood City Publishing

Redwood City, California

© 2007 Shannon Des Roches Rosa and Jennifer Byde Myers

Cover image © 2007 Lea Hernandez

All rights reserved

Library of Congress Control Number: 2007909327

ISBN 978-0-615-17796-0

First edition 2007

Manufactured in the United States of America

This is book is dedicated to our beautiful, quirky children

Gisela, Jack, Leo, India, and Kate,

and also to our husbands

Craig and Shawn,

who got to have so much bonus time with their kids

while this project swallowed us up.

STORIES

~~~~~~~~~~~~~~~~~~~~~

CAN I SIT WITH YOU?

Could more stress be crammed into fewer words? Though to some people this phrase means merely, "Yay, new friends," to a lot of us it brings sweaty palms, anxiety flashbacks, and the urge to crawl into a hole.

Dealing with the other kids at school is complicated even if you don't have a label. For those of us who are socially awkward, culturally juxtaposed, same-sex attracted, gender-cocooned, income-challenged, "weird" sibling-saddled, differently abled, atypical-looking, religiously isolated, on the autism spectrum, or who somehow just don't fit in, it can be brutal. Most of us eventually develop coping strategies; we grow up, leave elementary and junior high school, and try not to think about how much that time in our life sucked.

But then some of us started having our own kids, and saw those kids start fretting about how to fit in. Aiigh! What to do?

Well, we're not sure what most people would do, but we've decided to take action. We want to help our kids. We want to give them some ammunition, or at least some mental armor. We want to show them that almost everyone has been mystified or terrorized by the schoolyard social scene, though for different reasons and in different ways. We want them to see that their angst is both universal and timeless. We want them to know that other people totally understand.

So, we've collected some of our favorite writers' most memorable stories about surviving, succeeding, or sucking it up while dealing with the other kids at school. We've arranged them in the order in which they were first published on the Can I Sit With You? blog.

We think these stories encompass a wide range of experiences, but know that not everyone will find themselves reflected here. We suggest looking through the ever-increasing collection of stories on the Can I Sit With You? blog, www.canisitwithyou.org, or sending your own story to us at ciswysubmissions@gmail.com. We'd especially appreciate special needs themes, but all we really want are stories that go deep and ring true. We'll keep publishing stories as long as they keep coming in. And you can always discuss any of these stories by commenting on our blog.

We think you should know that this edition of the book serves a second purpose: proceeds from its sale directly benefit the Special Education Parent Teacher Association for Redwood City, California (SEPTAR, www.septar.org). SEPTAR works very hard to promote inclusive and tolerant school environments.

"Can I sit with you?" Well, we're hoping these stories might get just a few more kids to say, "Sure!" We wish this kind of acceptance for all of our children.

Shannon Des Roches Rosa and Jennifer Byde Myers
November 2007

Catching On

~~~~~~~~~~~~~~~~~~~~~

VICTORIA LARANETA
Age nine at the time

I went to a small grade school in the Midwest. Kickball was the favorite recess sport back in the 1950s. It was sort of like baseball, only without bats and with big heavy red rubber balls. I was always the kid who fell down on the way to school, or the clumsy girl who tripped on the stairs. At recess, when the team captains took turns picking the kids they wanted on their teams, I was always the last one standing:

"You take her!"

"No, you take her!"

That's what I always heard. It was like that for me all through junior high, and high school too.

When I was forty and I was trying to learn to play tennis, I realized what my problem was: I didn't have any hand-eye coordination. My tennis instructor helped me develop it, and sports became a whole new world.

I think it is pretty cool now when my husband throws me the car keys and I can catch them.

Bitch

~~~~~~~~~~~~~~~~~~~~~~~~

KATHLEEN CECCHIN
Seventh Grade

Lights up.

1976. A gaggle of seventh grade girls wearing dark green plaid wool skirts rolled up at the top so that they appear to be make-shift miniskirts, white short-sleeved blouses, white socks, and black shoes hang out in separate cliques of twos and threes in front of school doing the things that Catholic school girls do while waiting for the bell that summons them back to class after lunch: holding their school books, talking, laughing, gossiping, whispering, and screaming. Gangly, clumsy boys in white shirts, blue pants, and those ridiculous snap-on blue ties run about trying to push and punch each other and the girls, all in good fun. There is a distinct difference between the boys and girls that can only be explained by the fact that one group clearly hits puberty at least a year before the other.

Four girls make an entrance carrying a boom box playing a well-known '70s disco song that you can dance The Bump to. They are dressed in tight bell bottom jeans, tight shirts, and Converse gym shoes.

They wear heavy eyeliner, jewelry, and nail polish. They have no school books. Some have purses. They chew gum. Two girls trail the first group at a slight distance. They are dressed like the four girls, but lack their confidence and panache. They are obviously beta onlookers, and have accompanied the first group to witness the festivities.

All Catholic activity stops as the new girls walk over to two Catholic girls, form a line, and begin doing The Bump. The dancing continues for a beat or two until one of the girls, JANE, steps forward from the line. The line closes like the Red Sea behind her. They stop dancing. The music fades. JANE approaches one of the two Catholic girls.

JANE: "I heard you called me a *bitch*."

JANE mock-boxes the ears of the Catholic girl, quickly batting the girl's head back and forth between her hands. It is for effect rather than injury. The Catholic girl, arms full of books, makes no attempt to defend herself.

Suddenly, the Catholic girl throws her books up and behind her, knocking JANE's hands away. As papers fly, Catholics gasp and duck the school-book missiles. Meanwhile, the Red Sea opens at the center, pulls JANE behind the line, and closes again, separating JANE from the Catholic girl. JANE's group glares daringly at the Catholic girl.

The music rises as they turn and make their exit. They pass the two wannabes who giggle at the Catholic girl and then follow JANE and posse off left. The Catholics remain in place, stunned.

Lights down.

Sorry, Charlie

~~~~~~~~~~~~~~~~~~~~~~~

JENNIFER BYDE MYERS
Age nine at the time

In third grade I was in Mr. Lennon's class. It was a third/fourth grade mixed class at a segregated school for smarty-pants kids; I am quite certain we were all terrors in one way or another.

With special permission, third graders could stay later with the fourth graders to learn music. I loved to sing, and Mr. Lennon thought I had talent. I longed to perform in front of a crowd and watch people smile, so each time there was a solo, I felt compelled to audition. There were probably only three of us who could actually carry a tune: Amy Rosen, Kianna Wynters, and me. Amy was a sweet girl who was very shy. She accepted any role she was given, happy to be in or out of the spotlight. Kianna and I were best friends, and, as it turns out, arch rivals.

There wasn't a single activity I tried in which Kianna wasn't right there vying to be better or faster. Dodgeball got so competitive we ended up on opposing boys' fifth-grade teams. During the school Jogathon we completed an amazing 34 laps together. When I thought we were both done, Kianna ran away from me and completed another lap so she could "win." If I had a solo in the concert, she had a solo, even asking to add songs to the program if necessary. I never thought I was competing with Kianna until the activity was over and she would tell me how she had won. I guess it never mattered to me as long as we both did well and we were still best friends.

In May, Mr. Lennon decided we would put on a play for the entire school: You're a Good Man, Charlie Brown. Acting and singing! Performing in front of a paying audience! What could be better? I auditioned and got the part of Lucy. To cover my very blonde hair, I bought a black wig that night and made plans with my grandmother to make a blue dress. I was going to be an actress and Broadway was in my future. It was thrilling and I couldn't wait to start rehearsals.

There was only one problem: my best friend had no role in the play. There were props to be made, sets to design, and someone needed to be the prompter, hovering nearby if one of us forgot our lines. Kianna didn't sign up to do any of these other very important things because she insisted she should play the role of Lucy.

Kianna and her mom met privately with Mr. Lennon. Kianna made a petition asking that she be Lucy, and tried to get other kids to sign it. She even called my house and told me to tell the teacher I wasn't good enough at singing and should quit the play. On the playground Kianna let me know, in no uncertain terms, that I should give her the part since I "didn't even have black hair" and she did, naturally.

She told me that I was a horrible friend because I stole her part.

She told me I was selfish.

She claimed I had somehow cheated.

She wrote notes, folding them into tiny triangles: "I hate you."

I had no response for her. I was, for one of the few times in my life, stunned into silence. I could not imagine why she wasn't proud of me. I couldn't understand why she was being so hateful and mean. I wrote in my diary, "I'm so sad Kianna doesn't like me. We were BFFs and now, because of this stupid play, we aren't."

At home, I finally talked with my parents. Sobbing, I told them all of the things Kianna had said and done. I decided that, while the idea of being in the school play was one of the most exciting things I could ever imagine, having Kianna as my best friend maybe meant more. Since she was not going to be happy or be my friend if she wasn't Lucy, I had only one choice: give her the role.

My dad asked me, "Jenny, what would have happened if Kianna had gotten the part and you hadn't? Would you have been mad at her?"

My answer came right away. "No. It would have nothing to do with her. It would just mean that I wasn't good enough to do the part. I would be sad and disappointed, but why would I be mad at her?"

And it was like a light came on in my head. There was no way I was going to give up that part, and if Kianna wasn't going to be nice, it was her own problem. None of what she was doing had much to do with me. She was sad and disappointed, just like I would have been; she just didn't know that it wasn't my fault.

At school the next day, I wrote Kianna a note asking her to talk with me at lunch. We sat together and shared a pomegranate. I reminded her that we were best friends, which meant that she should be proud and happy for me to be Lucy. I also told her that it meant that I was sad and disappointed for her because she wasn't going to be on stage. I told her I wasn't going to quit the play, because even if I did, there was a chance that she still wouldn't be Lucy, and then neither of us would be happy.

It seemed to work. We hugged, and Kianna and I were inseparable once more. She helped me with my lines, and we decided that she would be the understudy, just in case I got a sore throat. She never said another mean thing about the play, and she even brought me a daisy on opening night.

(Oh, don't worry. Kianna got to "win" later. She was class president in eighth grade; I lost by nine votes.)

Best Friends

~~~~~~~~~~~~~~~~~~~~~

MARY TSAO
Fourth Grade

Fourth grade was not a good year for me. I was in a new school in a new town. The school I went to was in a wealthy neighborhood while I lived in a poorer neighborhood, which is another way of saying my family was poor while my classmates' families were not. Plus, I rode the bus to school, which at this school separated the kids who fit in from the kids who didn't. If your mom or dad drove you to school you fit in; if you rode the bus to school you didn't.

Oh, and did I mention that I had a buzz cut because the previous year I had head lice and my mom cut all my hair off? Yes, I was the new girl who had a bad haircut, wore the wrong clothes, lived in the wrong part of town, and rode the bus. All of those reasons combined with the fact that I was a shy, introverted kid who preferred reading books to playing sports or gossiping meant that I did not have many friends. And when I write that I did not have many friends, I mean that I had no friends at all.

But one day all of that changed. On that day, a cute little girl with short brown hair, a smattering of freckles across her nose, and a squeaky voice, decided that she wanted to be my friend, my best friend. I had a friend! I started to like going to school.

My friend and I met up in the schoolyard after the bus dropped me off. We talked about life, and she confided in me that she was trying to stop biting her nails. She showed me how she coated her chewed-up nails in a mixture of hot sauce and vinegar so that she wouldn't be inclined to bite them. She said it hurt her fingers and that she was growing to like the taste of hot sauce, but I was impressed. She was the first person I knew who was actively trying to improve herself. She seemed so mature.

She also had the kind of family life that I dreamed of having: the kind with a mother and a father, a brother, and a dog. I lived with my single mom and my twin sister; I idolized anybody who had the things I didn't have. She introduced me to the concept of talking on the phone, and one night we talked for hours. I ended up getting in trouble because my mom's boyfriend kept getting a busy signal when he called our house, but it was worth it. I had a friend.

Until the day I went to school and she had a new friend. That was the day she told me that she and the other girl had discussed it, and they had decided that best friends don't come in threes. I was the odd girl out. Literally. And with those harsh words spoken in a matter-of-fact tone and before the first bell rang, I no longer had a friend.

I don't remember how long our friendship lasted. I don't think it was very long. I don't remember the girl's name or much about her except for what I've told you. The thing I remember most vividly is how

Can I Sit With You?

she put hot sauce on her fingers. Looking back, it seems appropriate that a girl who liked hurting herself—even if it was in the name of self-improvement—would think nothing of hurting me.

It was difficult, but I managed to survive fourth grade. I kept to myself, read a lot of books, and buried myself in imaginary worlds where best friends were reliable and if they weren't, justice was swiftly served.

I went to a different school for fifth grade and for various reasons, my life improved. I had several close friends and I didn't feel as alone, different, or isolated as I did in fourth grade. I never did get another best girlfriend, though. Having one best friend in a lifetime is enough for me.

Love Hurts

~~~~~~~~~~~~~~~~~~~~~~

SARAH M. GLOVER

Age ten at the time

Mark Grady disfigured my back for life. Mark Grady. Even after thirty-odd years, the name still makes me cringe in agony. Mark Grady—a sadist, a scoundrel, and a bully. I loved him. Desperately.

Fifth grade. For me boys were nothing but chimps with less fur. Dirty nails. Dirty necks. No redeemable qualities. Except for Mark Grady, curse his lanky, green-eyed soul.

It all started innocently in Mrs. Cotoia's class.

"Should men learn how to cook and clean?" she asked. Mrs. Cotoia was a feminist. She wore cool bell bottoms and hoop earrings. She looked like she should have a theme song.

We wide-eyed girls nodded rapidly.

The boys grumbled—the few that were paying attention at all. Except Mark Grady. He held up his hand. His clean, sculptured hand connected to his white oxford-shirted arm which led to his perfect shoulders. He smiled. I felt my heart move to my throat and beat so loudly I thought it might pop out onto my desk and quiver its way to him frantically, leaving a slimy trail. Bump, bump. Lurch. Bump, bump. Lurch.

"Mrs. Cotoia," he said, wistfully, "Women are supposed to take care of men. I mean, I don't see why we need to do that when it's not our job. That's what my dad says."

My teacher's lips pursed so, her face appeared inside out. His face remained angelic. I imagined a room full of aunts squeezing that face till it turned blue.

"Are you crazy?" I shouted, coming to the aid of my teacher, intent to strike a blow for women everywhere. "Who'd want to take care of you? You better learn how to cook or else you're going to starve and your house is going pile up with junk and nobody's gonna clean it. You think we're on this earth just to serve you?" My face burned and fire filled my eyes. Mrs. Cotoia beamed. Mark Grady's hand descended, his eyes narrowing. Recess was only a breath away. Vengeance simmered in his stare.

I went out to the playground. I grabbed my best friend Elise's hand, determined to move as far from my enemy as possible. The swings seemed the safest bet. They would offer visibility and a quick method of escape if necessary. Elise took the seat next to me and I adjusted my wrap-skirt. We pumped our legs in unison until we were soaring high up into the sky. The wind felt good on my bare legs. I watched it blow the dirt and rocks below our feet into swirling clumps.

"You know," shouted Elise, "You're probably in love."

"What?"

"With Mark Grady. Even with the yelling—the way you drool over him in class. It's love. Definitely. Right?"

"Shhhhh!" I pumped my legs a few more times to calm my frantic heart. Within minutes, I had confessed to her the deepest and most passionate secrets of my heart.

Then I heard laughing. I looked up. Mark Grady was leaning against the school, laughing. He had heard everything. I just knew it! Mortification flooded my veins. I slung low in the swing to hide my face from his sight. I slipped backwards; the swing caught my knees as I cringed with horror.

"Please, please God, don't let him have heard!"

On the downswing, the entire length of my back raked across the dirt and rocks below, tearing the flesh down my spine like a giant cheese grater. My skirt flew up over my head, exposing my bottom. The pain that stabbed like knives through my skin was nothing compared to the horror of having my underwear on display for the world to see. The world and Mark Grady. I screamed. The entire playground turned. I couldn't right myself. I flailed like a beached whale. My back scraped across the rocks again. I roared. Somehow, I flung my body over my knees and landed with a crash onto the dirt, skinning my hands and knees.

In the blur of the next few moments, a crowd of eager students, thrilled at the sight of that much blood, surrounded me. I was sobbing now; big gooey globs of snot and tears smeared with the dirt on my knees.

"What happened? What happened?" yelled Mrs. Cotoia's voice. She kneeled down next to me. "Jesus, Mary, and Joseph!"

Her tone made me howl. Girls cringed in wide-eyed alarm. Boys snickered. Elise was hyperventilating.

Mrs. Cotoia composed herself and tried to gather me in her arms. "What happened? Did you fall?"

I was crying too much to answer. My pigtails were glued to my cheeks.

"What happened?" Mrs. Cotoia repeated sternly.

"It's not her fault," cried Elise in my defense. "She wants Mark Grady to kiss her and marry her and have babies with her and doesn't want him to know so she fell back on her swing so he wouldn't see her face then her back scraped against the rocks and that's why she's bleeding!"

A scandalous hush blanketed the playground. My life was over. I could fall into the blood- and snot-filled dirt, curl up, and die. They could put flowers over my body where other ostracized children could come and pay their respects, like some Lourdes for losers.

Eventually, bodies drifted away, giggling and snickering. Mrs. Cotoia lifted me in her arms. "We need to get you to the nurse," she whispered. My back burned with each step as we trudged the long stretch back to school alone.

"There is one thing you need to know."

I looked up into her kind eyes, wiping my nose with my arm. "What?"

I followed her gaze to where Mark Grady sat with his friends on a picnic table, tossing a softball into the air and roaring in laughter.

"Scars can happen anywhere. Inside and out. And both can hurt."

My back stung terribly as I watched him sit there, smug and cruel. I sniffed. "You're wrong. The scars on the inside hurt ... more."

My Sister

~~~~~~~~~~~~~~~~~~~~~~

JACKIE OLSEN
Third Grade

In elementary school my sister seemed to sail along unscathed, whereas I was subject to any number of indignities from my classmates on a regular basis.

To my sister, I was a pest, a trial, a barnacle on the side of her gloriously perfect ship. It was horrifying and vexing by turns to be that little sister. I couldn't get it together no matter what I did. I was always late, always making her late, always forgetting something, or breaking something else.

My sister did her best to duck out of walking me home from school, pointing out that, at eight years old, I was able to ride my bike home by myself. It certainly suited her to not have to deal with her pesky little sister.

In third grade I was plagued by two boys who made fun of me almost constantly. Nothing my parents did seemed to stop the abuse. One day, the two boys laid in wait for me on the way home from school.

I was riding home fast, standing up on the pedals to get up the hills. Suddenly something sailed by, and there they were, running up to me on the bike, throwing something at me. Eggs! I was being egged. One hit my arm and splattered over my shirt. I rode harder and made it around the corner, and was soon home.

My sister was in the kitchen, and turned from the stove to see me stagger into the house with tears in my eyes. "What! What happened!" she asked.

"They egged me," I cried. "Eggs. They threw eggs at me."

And wouldn't you know it, my sister turned out to have at least one sympathetic bone in her body. She vowed to get those boys for me. "I'll ride home with you tomorrow," she said. I soon calmed myself at the prospect of my big sister helping me out.

The next day it snowed, hard. The sky was white and we walked home from school together.

From out of the white came the boys. "Hey, fathead," said one of them. (I'd been called "fathead" all year, despite my using the great comeback line, "fat heads have big brains." Like that helped. They just didn't let up, those boys.)

My sister froze in place. I looked desperately at her as the boys drew closer, snowballs in hand. At least it wasn't eggs this time around. But she wouldn't be any help at all, I could tell. I summoned my courage.

I yelled, "Think of an *ice cold shower*," sneering. "Imagine the *ice cold water*." They stared at me. "You're covered in *ice cold*." In the moment I couldn't think of anything else to say, but I used what little I had.

We pushed through and ran, and they didn't throw the snowballs until we were halfway down the block.

"I can't believe you did that," said my sister. I couldn't help noticing just a little bit of admiration in her voice. Ah, the triumph.

MEN-STRU-A-TION

~~~~~~~~~~~~~~~~~~~~~~

JUDY McCRARY KOEPPEN
Junior High

For many, junior high is a time characterized by gawky looks, lanky extremities, braced teeth, and questionable skin clarity. But even those fortunate enough to have a proportionate body, naturally straight teeth, and even skin tone cannot escape the Big P.

Puberty. A time in life when hormones invade and one's body begins to morph and alienate its owner. Adding injury to the hormonal insult is the obsessive desire by girls to be carbon copies of their peers. Well, that's the way it was for me. I spent every moment certain that everyone was looking at me. I just knew the eyes of the world watched, and were interested in the exact length of my pants, if my hair was brushed, and if my lips were glossed. When one lives in a perpetual state of self-absorption, the most embarrassing horrors are often caused by one's self.

My November birthday made me older than most of my peers. In addition, I was an early bloomer. Though my breast buds were size

AA at best, no matter; I was sure my voluptuous tatas turned the corner and entered a room an hour before the rest of my body. The embarrassment of my body embracing its early spring was further fueled by my mother's insistence on using appropriate and anatomically correct terms. Three and four syllable words were stretched and articulated nearly beyond recognition.

"Oh that's great! You are MEN-STRU-A-TING!"

"Do you need any more SAN-I-TA-RY NAP-KINS?"

"Are your BREASTS tender?"

"Are your NIP-PLES feeling sensitive?"

"Is your VA-GI-NA bothering you?"

In my junior high era, girls didn't carry purses, or at least I certainly didn't. Kids also didn't haul backpacks from class to class. No one used a tampon back then; certainly, no one even admitted to having crossed over to womanhood. All this made it difficult to safely secure and hide a SAN-I-TA-RY NAP-KIN. (Now, of course, I called them "pads," not nearly so offensive a word.)

Following lunch one day, I decided to change my pad in the girls' locker room bathroom just before P.E. But how could I carry a pad from my outdoor locker to the locker room? There were no pockets in my light blue Dittos jeans. No matter that it was 95 degrees, I donned my lemon-yellow windbreaker and slipped the contraband into the pocket. I stepped into the swarms of moving students and headed to P.E.

I can still picture it. I was ten feet from the entrance to the girls' locker room. Suddenly, my not-so-mini pad dove out from under the lemon-yellow hem. It was a slow motion event. It was then that I remembered the fist-sized rip in my pocket.

After escaping, the pad jumped on a current created by all the moving bodies. It dashed left, glided right, swirled above a light-brown Wallaby shoe, dipped down, and finally came to rest on the sizzling concrete. I couldn't breathe. I wanted to run, but I was fixed to the spot. Should I pick it up? Should I kick it under the bush? Should I just ignore it and run? I decided to go with ignoring it entirely.

I regrouped, cloaked myself in my best casual saunter, and slipped into the girls' locker room. I was certain that from that moment on, everyone in the entire school knew, and cared, that I was MEN-STRU-A-TING.

Forever Young

~~~~~~~~~~~~~~~~~~~~~

ELAINE PARK
Elementary School

For a few years, in grades five and six, I went to a small rural school a few miles from a town that was a few hundred miles from anywhere else. At lunch and recess we all played marbles and the girls skipped rope. I could manage single-rope skipping, but never double dutch. I was not even allowed to turn the ropes for double dutch. In the winter we played a game that involved tramping out a big circle in the snow, cut into pie-shaped pieces that we had to run around. We played dodgeball, which I was relatively good at, although to this day I am uncomfortable with things flying at my head. The kids teased me for coloring people's hair orange when I was doing art, but I was pretty sure that "red hair" was just a figure of speech and the orange crayon was the way to go.

By seventh grade, I was discovered to be an advanced learner and got sent into town on the bus to Robert Moore Elementary, the biggest school in the area. We had French taught to us by a hip young Québécois couple who were eventually caught smoking dope and fired. We had music taught to us by the crusty high school band teacher and learned to play recorders.

The students at Robert Moore were contemptuous of "farmers," as they called us kids who came in on the bus. Although some of the kids did live on farms, the label didn't make sense for me. We had moved to the area from an even more remote northwestern Ontario town, but before that we had lived in England, France, and Belgium, as my dad was in the military police in the Canadian Air Force. I had seen the gondolas of Venice, walked among the row-on-row crosses in Verdun, gone shoe shopping in London, and gotten my first pair of glasses in Luxembourg. I had learned to say "fermez la bouche" courtesy of the rude grandchildren of the lady who lived next door to us in the village of Virton. My parents were both from Toronto, and my mother was painfully intellectual and only listened to classical music and Broadway musicals. She had a lifetime birding list. Clearly, it was not I who was the hick.

When I first started going to school at Robert Moore, some of the kids tried to set me up for a prank involving a boy who was overweight. They crafted a pretend love note from him to me. It was going to be a masterful humiliation doubleheader. The girl who sat behind me (and who a few years later became quite a nice person) passed me the note. I somehow picked up the wrong piece of paper and opened it up. It was blank. "That piece of paper you passed me was blank," I earnestly told her. Much later I found the pretend love note and realized with some wonder that I had completely messed up the plan, basically by confusing everyone too much to proceed.

After a while, though, I developed some solid credibility by being compulsively defiant of any form of authority while pulling down some of the highest marks in the school, and also by being a little exotic from having lived abroad. I was welcomed to join the bad kids in the back alley while they smoked cigarettes, even though I didn't smoke myself. I eventually became part of a group of girls who liked me as much as I liked them, and we stuck together from then on.

I'm sure I wasn't happy about any teasing I endured during these years, but when I look back, I don't remember feeling that angry or bitter about it. I knew I was an outsider, but I changed school every two years until I got to high school, so I was an outsider for a legitimate reason. I also took my status as evidence of my superiority. I was proud of being different because being different for me meant being better.

Instead, when I think about it all, I feel a softly glowing gratitude for the kids who did befriend me. There was the girl who taught me how to draw a face by making a U and then filling in the details of hair and eyes and nose. The girl who came to my house to make mud pies and act out episodes of The Man From Uncle, and who joined me on a tour of all the town's churches one day when there was no adult around to stop us. The girl who had me over to her crowded, noisy house where the only place to find solitude was on the roof of her porch. The neighborhood gang who included me in a perpetual traveling game of football that raced from yard to yard on summer afternoons. The tangles of kids who absorbed me as a matter of course into the jumping, swinging, chasing anarchy of childhood fun.

I especially remember with satisfaction the friends who were along with me on the wild ride from grade seven dances to graduation day. It's been a long, long time since I've seen or heard from them. I guess I could find them if I wanted to, find them graying, and matronly, and slightly disapproving of me and my habit of running for freedom whenever obligation gets too close. But I prefer to keep them as they were, especially my closest and best friend, who lives forever in my mind with her long, brown hair blowing behind her in overlapping flaps as she bikes ahead of me, sensible, loyal, and kind—with friends and family intact and the whole glorious future stretching out in front of her—it's a memory that I treasure and don't want to redeem for the unequal reality of the present. I hold it as a sacred icon—for me and for her.

Wet Dog

~~~~~~~~~~~~~~~~~~~~~~

LAURA (HENRY) KUKULSKI
Seventh Grade

In seventh grade I was going through a major awkwardness phase. Okay, who wasn't? I was on the brink of figuring out how to assert myself and promote my own personality, but still followed the lead of a few more obnoxious girls from my elementary school days. I wore big, ugly, thick glasses, had a hideous Ogilvie home perm (thanks, Mom) and was a short, shy, bookworm nerd.

Then a new girl, Becky, moved in to our neighborhood one street over from me. She was a year older and was huge, thuggish, and played soccer. Somehow she became friends with my best friend, yet at the same time made my life a living hell on the bus to school every day. I was no stranger to being taunted on the bus, but she was in my face, yelling and scary. She would call me a "wet dog" when I got on the bus with wet hair in the morning. My friends did not defend me. My sense of outrage—that this big, stupid, mulleted, new girl could come and completely disrupt my life—grew and grew.

One day, during my bus ride home, I waited for Becky to get off the bus, then screamed, "You're a bitch!" out the window at her. I sat back down and knew my life was over. I could hear her screaming back, "You're dead! I am going to kick your ass tomorrow!"

I got off the bus one stop later and ran home so I could barricade myself inside. I was trembling, crying, and sick with dread. I was going to have to be in a fight. What would it be like? It would hurt and I would have to try to punch her back.

I can't remember anything until the end of the next school day. I was at my locker getting my books and all of the sudden there was a huge crowd of people behind me, yelling. Becky was there yelling at me; another girl, Kelly, yelled at me to take my glasses off so that Becky could punch me. Someone grabbed my books out of my hands and threw them over the lockers. It was all a hideous confused blur. I started yelling that there was no way I was going to take off my glasses so that someone could hit me, were they idiots? I started crying and somehow managed to push my way out of the crowd to a bunch of teachers who were standing nearby.

I tried to tell a teacher what had happened. One of them grabbed my arm above the elbow, hard, and dragged me to where my books had been thrown. She made me pick them up and then dragged me to the vice principal's office. I kept asking her to let go of me, and said she was hurting me. I told her I had not thrown my own books (why would I throw my own books, lady?), that someone else had, and that they had tried to hit me. Outrage! She did not listen and she did not care and neither did the vice principal.

I got three days of in-school suspension. (Why?) Becky attempted to become my best friend, inviting me over to play PlayStation (not interested!) and filling up my locker with candy and cake and balloons.

The girl picking on me, the teacher, the crowd of kids—none of their behavior made sense to me. This is one of the incidents that really helped me realize that: a) I could defend myself b) I didn't have to be friends with anyone I didn't really like and c) other people were idiots and it wasn't my problem.

The Flipside

~~~~~~~~~~~~~~~~~~~~~~

KATRINA N. MUELLER

Age twelve at the time

In the middle of my fourth grade year my family moved to small town Idaho. I got made fun of from the very first day, so naturally, I made friends with the only person geekier than I was. But I still tentatively sought approval from my peers—and got rejected, of course. I was the new kid. This didn't truly bother me until sixth grade.

At the beginning of that year I had only one friend—the same friend I'd had since I arrived. Jon M. He had a horrible temper with everyone but me. His family was poor and couldn't afford things like toothpaste, so his teeth were awful. He was the shortest kid in class. But he was so very smart, and a naturally talented flute player. He taught me how to play checkers, and how to pump your legs hard enough on the swings to achieve Warp Speed Nine.

Sixth grade was the year I lost him.

For some reason, the girls in my class took pity on me. They tried to make me over, make me "cool" just like them. I could hardly believe it.

I was finally being accepted! The only problem was, they told me that I couldn't hang out with Jon anymore. In fact, I had to make fun of him just like they did or else I wouldn't be a part of the group.

Peer pressure is one of the most horrible things on the planet. I caved in. I became one of the bullies. I made fun of Jon. I still remember the look on his face when I did it. It killed me. I couldn't believe I'd done that to my one true friend.

The next year, when we started seventh grade, I wanted to apologize to him. My eyes constantly roamed the halls, looking for my friend, but I never saw him again. His sister told me he was being home schooled because he "didn't have any friends at school anymore."

I will never forget my friend Jon, and how I lost him. I work hard every day to be kind to people, in the hope that someday I will be able to forgive myself.

Love Is the Best Revenge

~~~~~~~~~~~~~~~~~~~~

TAMMY HARRISON
Sixth Grade

In 1975, my childhood ended and my life became a mess; beyond a mess, really. It was a mess that I had no control or say-so over. My dad became hospitalized after an aneurysm burst in the back of his brain, and my mother was incapable of caring for herself, let alone her five children (but she tried!). After fighting with one of Dad's brothers to keep her children, she moved us all back to our hometown to live with her.

Mom attempted to be both a mother and a father to us. She got us enrolled in school and things started appearing normal again. I was in the sixth grade. Dad was still recovering in the hospital.

But there was a girl in my class who didn't like me, for some reason. Glenda. To this day, I still have no idea why. I rarely talked, as I was painfully introverted because of my family life. I had no friends in my class as all of my neighborhood friends were either older, younger, or went to other schools.

Glenda was just flat-out mean. And I was a prime target for her anger because I didn't talk back and didn't fight back.

She'd walk into class every morning, and there I'd be, sitting at my desk. If the teacher wasn't in the room, or if she had her back turned, Glenda would tower over me, and pummel me. Right in front of everyone. She pounded on my head and arms. No one laughed. No one helped. They just watched, and when Glenda was done, she went to her desk and sat down as if nothing had happened.

I did nothing.

My parents were both abusive alcoholics, which means that when they drank beer, they got mean and beat each other up. I'd lived a life of people hitting each other—all the time. If it wasn't my parents fighting, it was one of my brothers fighting. Or my aunts and uncles. At my young age, I thought that if Mom would just quit fighting back, she'd spare herself a lot of pain, bruises, and unexplained hospital visits.

So, I sat there and took my beating from Glenda, every school day from August through February of my sixth grade school year.

One morning in February, the hospital called and said that Dad was gone. Mom gathered us around and told us he'd died. We cried because she was crying, but he'd been gone from our home for six months already, and we'd already gotten used to not having him around.

I missed school for a few days to attend the funeral.

The morning I returned to school, I sat at my desk waiting for my daily torture session from Glenda.

It didn't happen.

Instead, on my desk was a packet of sympathy cards from my classmates (including one from Glenda). I don't remember what they said, or even what hers said. All I know is that from that day on, Glenda left me alone. She never raised another fist to me. I suppose she figured the pain I was now feeling from the loss of my dad was enough for her, and she'd moved on to hurt someone else. Thankfully, we went to different junior high schools.

Within three months of my dad's death, my mother got tired of his family's interference in our lives and she abandoned us. (Left us! My mother left her children while we were at school. I still can't believe it, over 30 years later.) I was put into foster homes since I refused to live with my dad's family, who had taken my sister and three brothers. Mom committed suicide the next year, because the family wouldn't let her have her children back. She killed herself because she couldn't love her kids again.

I was lucky though, because I had my Gramma from Tramma. She was my mom's mother, and she and I had a very special relationship. She loved me like no one else did and she treated me as if I were the princess in her castle.

It would seem everything was okay, but I still had that old resentment towards Glenda. In my mind I still needed retribution, retaliation, and revenge. She hurt me when I was already hurting. She beat me when I was already down. She could not have cared less about my feelings, or my soul. I thought I would never be free of my feelings towards her until I let her have it, once and for all.

I played basketball in the ninth grade. Our school happened to play her school. And there, walking into the gym, cocky and excited with pre-game anticipation, was Glenda. I'll never forget the way I felt when she came into my view. I was no longer the introverted, gotta-take-someone-else's-punishment type of person. I had overcome a lot of issues, especially after defying my dad's family and living where I wanted to live. I wasn't taking anyone else's crap anymore. Glenda's included.

But, guess what? Glenda didn't remember me! She didn't give me a second look. She was still mouthy and still a thug, but she didn't single me out, because she didn't even remember me. This told me she'd treated many others the same way she treated me—and she was so self-confident that she felt she was above reproach.

When we went to the locker room for half-time the coach gave us a pep talk. He happened to mention something about Glenda and how she'd had a tough life, that she was a fighter on and off the court and that we were to stop her, but carefully because she played rough. She came from a broken home, and ran around getting into fights and even in trouble with the law, because she didn't have anyone who cared about her.

With those words, I suddenly felt lucky. I had love from my very special Gramma; love that would stay with me forever and ever—and Glenda didn't!

I smiled a very smug smile, knowing that Glenda's tough life was payback enough. I didn't need to lift a finger or say a mean word to her. Nope, I just stood there with a smile that never left my face for the rest of the game. I didn't need to take action against her. I didn't have to hurt her, or myself.

When I went home, I called my Gramma, and thanked her for loving me.

Junior High

~~~~~~~~~~~~~~~~~~~~

ANONYMOUS

Sixth Grade

My best friend Alison and I had a lot of fun together after school and on weekends. We rode bikes around the neighborhood, went to Thrifty for ice cream and to try on makeup, and talked on the phone for hours. Our birthdays were a day apart, our senses of humor were compatible, and we both loved Judy Blume, prank phone calls, and sleep away camp. But she shared her actual birth date with Wendi, a girl in the popular crowd.

In seventh grade, Alison and Wendi planned a joint birthday party—a night-time party with boys, dancing, and who knows what else. I write "who knows" because I wasn't there. I wasn't invited.

Alison explained that she couldn't invite me because she didn't want Wendi and her crowd to know that we were friends. She said she could only act friendly to me outside of school—otherwise I'd blow her cover. Pretty terrible, no? Unfortunately, my self-esteem was, too, because I accepted the terms of her friendship. I just wanted to keep her as a friend. The night of the Alison/Wendi party, I stayed home and cried in my room.

Last time I checked, Alison and Wendi hadn't talked since the eighties. Alison never was fully accepted into Wendi's dominant popular clique, but she found her own group in high school. I had my own group too. We did stay friends, though.

And believe it or not, I am still friendly with Alison. Am I able to maintain the friendliness because I am happy with my spouse, kids, work, and life, and she is single and hates her job? Maybe! Wheel of Karma?

My daughter can't believe that someone would do that to me. I am so glad she is indignant about it. I don't think she'd put up with Alison's terms. I am glad she is stronger and has more self-esteem than I did!

First Grade Reader

~~~~~~~~~~~~~~~~~~~~~

JENIFER SCHARPEN

Age six at the time

My first grade teacher was maybe not the most insightful woman to ever pass out a Dick and Jane reader, and I really don't remember many things about the days I spent in her classroom. I do remember though, what divided me from my classmates and made it impossible for me to have any friends: I could read.

I started first grade when I was five, but just weeks away from turning six. My parents had (rightfully) convinced the school district to let me jump over kindergarten because I could already read and write without much help. If my father were telling this part of the story, he'd point out that I liked to read him the newspaper, and that I spoke using perfect grammar from the time I was tiny until the end of that first week of school. (The grammar didn't stand a chance once I was hanging around with actual children.)

There were two other kids in first grade who could read: Deborah and Michael. We sat huddled together in the back corner of the classroom with our pencils, books, and Big Chief tablets, away from the kids who were learning the basics.

This, of course, was bad. You'd think that we'd have had each other, but even my socially-challenged brain figured out that we were so uncool and unwelcome it would be best to act like the other kids and just hate each other and ourselves. Especially since our teacher loved to use us as examples for the class: "Someday you'll be reading like they are!"

I remember sitting at my desk on one of the first days of school and watching a kid cut up his lunch money, a dollar, with his safety scissors. He did a great job, ending up with tiny and even squares. I was horrified. Somehow it seemed worse to me than cutting up an American flag (which I likened it to at the time) and I knew I had to tell. I did. And the kid was sent back to kindergarten. Thirty-one years later I still feel guilty.

Peeing my pants at the zoo didn't exactly help my social standing, either. Nor did the fact that I was so small and so allergy riddled and so, so freckled. But, I think what really did me in was my job as classroom monitor.

I still dream about it. I had to stand up on a chair parked by the chalkboard at the head of the class. I held a thin piece of chalk in my hand and my instructions were to write down the name of any child who talked. The teacher would leave the room and give me this look. This look that was like, "Okay, you are totally more responsible and mature than these other kids. You're just a small adult. So, help me out, give me a break from this and do my job for me so I can go out for a smoke." I may be misinterpreting this memory a little, but the next part is unforgettable: the sound of kids talking and laughing loud enough to be heard through the classroom door. The closed classroom door. The classroom door through which I could hear the teacher's shoes clomping down the tile hallway.

Talk about damned if you do and damned if you don't.

I don't remember what I did. Sometimes there's a flash of the teacher demanding to know who was talking, but I really don't know what happened. Probably, I tattled. At least the teacher seemed to admire me and I sure didn't want to lose that.

One time during the school year a girl from my class asked me to play. "Come with me," she'd said, dragging me by the shirtsleeve. We ended up underneath a tree near the seesaw and the chain link fence and the street. "Bury my hands in the dirt," she commanded, "look down close at them now." I was fascinated and did as I was told. I figured it out only when I saw the flash of her hands flinging the dirt into my face. And of course that was too late. It wasn't bad enough that everyone thought I was weird and a teacher's pet. Now I had dirt in my eyes and in my mouth and up my nose.

Still, I remember the day that I did come home with that Dick and Jane reader. I remember my parents being happy for me, telling me that they'd read it when they were little, too. I remember showing it to them as we walked through the parking lot of the apartment complex where we lived. I remember taking it out and looking at it as I walked home from school. I knew it was cool to be able to read.

I knew first grade wouldn't last forever.

Political Ambitions

~~~~~~~~~~~~~~~~~~~~~

LINDA SASLOW
Junior High

In elementary school and junior high school, I was never a popular child. I was the smart kid. I was the wise cracker in the gifted kids' MGM program, the one everyone resented because academics came easily to me. Perhaps I raised my hand too much. Knowing too many answers was never a character trait that the other children liked. Plus, I was horrible at sports.

In sixth grade—the year was about 1980—I wrote an essay about how I wanted to be the first woman president. This is a reality it seems I will not achieve now that it is 2007, I am 37 and there is a viable female candidate for the top office of the land. The essay was printed in the school yearbook. I got some sort of prize at an assembly. My parents and teachers liked the essay. My peers did not.

In seventh grade, I decided to take the bull by the horns and run for student council. I wanted to be vice president. My father thought this was a grand idea. The problem was that I was not one of the popular children. My mother bought me gingham dresses and I willingly wore them to school. I was still smart, but my friends were few. I was in no way cool. I didn't have the right clothes and I did not listen to the right music. My hair was hopeless. My mother would only take me to her friend for haircuts, and that friend would never do the short, fashionable styles I desired.

My father helped me make posters to hang at Goddard Junior High School in Glendora, California. The signs were cute with hand-drawn cartoon characters. I wrote some sort of speech and was incredibly nervous when I had to deliver it to the entire student body at a podium in the gym.

I did not win.

I was bummed about my defeat for a while, but then I realized I was still one of the smart kids, even if I could not win a popularity contest. There were places for me to fit in.

In eighth grade, I became the editor of the junior high newspaper, which was still run off on an archaic mimeograph machine. Even a photocopier was too high tech for the newspaper office in 1982. I was a good writer before becoming editor of the paper, but I really started to shine once I had acknowledgment for my work. Plus, I had a staff, some of the kids were popular, and they had to kiss up to me to get their stories printed. This I liked. I had the power that I craved. But I had been appointed by teachers, not put up to a popular vote.

For my thirteenth birthday my mother let me have a large party in the back yard. It was a co-party with a friend who was a bit more popular, so I had hopes that some of the cool kids would come. My friend's mom made a cake and my mother bought one of those really long sub sandwiches. Everyone came. I was amazed. I was suddenly no longer a pariah.

Eighth grade proved to be much better for me, socially. I had lunch friends. I was on an AYSO soccer team. I discarded the gingham dresses for jeans and corduroy pants. My mother finally allowed me to pick out my own clothes. I got my ears pierced.

At the end of eighth grade I decided to try out for cheerleader. I was nervous during the audition, and I was not picked to be a freshman cheerleader. It seemed that true popularity would always elude me.

At the end of my thirteenth year, I moved to another city, hours away. I had to find my way in a whole new social environment. I was never especially popular in high school, but I managed to make newspaper editor again, and had a small circle of genuine friends.

I just watched my oldest child wade through junior high, and became acutely aware again how twelve- and thirteen-year-olds are especially cruel. The competition to be thin, have good hair, and trendy clothes has not changed a bit. I doubt it ever will.

Lose and Win

~~~~~~~~~~~~~~~~~~~~~~

JACKIE DAVIS-MARTIN
Junior High

The last parade of the summer carried me on highs and lows like those of the giant Ferris wheel dominating Kennywood Park, the magical scene of our annual marching band competition. It was 1955 and I was thirteen years old, equally preoccupied with garnering another victory for our junior high band, and trying to get a boy I really liked to pay attention to me.

We scrambled off the buses on the evening of the competition. The roller coasters undulated seductively around the parking lot where we were assigned to line up. I tried to concentrate on the parade route that Mr. Girotta, our director, was explaining to me, while keeping track of the boy I liked, Beanie. I was hoping to go on the rides with him afterward, my heart pounding already at the possibility of being buckled in next to him, of our being thrust with force against each other rounding the roller coaster curves, our arms shooting skyward in simultaneous joy.

Mr. Girotta followed my gaze and smiled. "Yeah, that's what I want to talk to you about. Beanie's on bass drum tonight."

Our regular drummer was sick, he told me, frowning. Mr. Girotta had been teaching and drilling us kids since fourth grade and took us everywhere to compete. I was the drum major (or "-ette" as we added back then), sort of his right-hand girl, a position of both honor and isolation. As "major of the drum," my job was to cue in the bass drum at times of playing opportunities, for instance while passing a judges' stand. I got to wear a skirted costume with gold braid, a furry hat and tasseled boots, and carry a big fancy baton. I would hold that baton high and blow my whistle. Then, the drums' rat-a-tatting would shift to the bass drum's BOOM-boom! BOOM-boom! BO-O-O-O-M, BOOM-boom! The band would play! I knew that the worst thing that could happen to a school band was to march in muted cadence past the judges' stand, instruments smartly and uselessly tucked under armpits.

Mr. Girotta stressed that the problem was to bring the band around the wide arc of the merry-go-round just before the judges' stand. He left, and I crossed the dusty lot to Beanie, who, although he made my heart flutter, was a wild card in the reliability department.

Beanie was tall and skinny and didn't take much seriously. He had just moved here at the end of seventh grade, and everyone liked him. His spaghetti-like arms would wave above the snares or the triangles, or even, occasionally, on the cymbals. At one concert, before the curtain went up, he actually dropped a cymbal, sending all of us into muffled paroxysms of laughter. When the cymbal circled upon itself in resounding layers of clamor, Beanie scrunched up his eyes in a wincing apology.

"Hi, Miss Boss Lady," he greeted me. I cringed; I wanted then to be a cute third clarinetist, in pants, with no concerns. "Mr. G. told me about the stand and all. I know what to do."

"Oh! Good!" was all I could gasp. Then, ever Mr. Girotta's emissary, I couldn't resist, "Beanie, your top button isn't buttoned."

He gaped at me. "My what? My button? Oh, well, pardon me!" He buttoned it up with elaborate gestures, his skinny elbows jutting wide. "Aha!" (He took a step back.) "What do I see here?" (He glanced at my white boots.) "Dust! Your boots have dust on them, Miss Perfect."

I almost started to cry. "I'm not that at all," I said. Did all this mean he liked me, or he didn't? "You'll watch me, won't you? You know the signal?" I waved my clunky wand in the air, demonstrating.

He leaned forward, close enough to kiss. "I won't take my eyes off you!" he said, smiling, then straightened to buckle on his drum.

I tested Beanie early on. Our band was arranged in seven rows of seven, the percussion in the fourth row, bass drum in the middle. The first time I signaled, he boomed the roll-off, the band played its rousing Thunderer march. I felt on top of the world. I signaled near Kiddieland, then the Ferris wheel, and twice more. We were a team, Beanie and I! I strutted confidently toward the merry-go-round, pumping the baton.

But suddenly, the cadence grew fainter, and then got lost in the calliope music. I blew the whistle hard, and flourished the baton. Nothing happened. I did it again. Again, nothing. I turned around with the worst feeling, and realized that I had lost most of the band! Still with me were two rows of clarinets and flutes, looking over their shoulders nervously, and then there was a separation—a big space—that stretched around the merry-go-round into some unknown Hell I didn't want to think about.

The piccolo player pointed beyond me, and I glanced over my shoulder to see that I was also losing our connection to the rest of the parade.

I pranced over to the lost rows of the band, blowing my whistle hysterically. Nothing! I stopped and screamed, "Roll Off! Take the Roll Off!" This was so far beyond protocol that even now I cringe.

BOOM-boom! BOOM-boom! BO-O-O-O-M, BOOM-boom! Finally. I ran in high phony marches back to where I was supposed to be, to the strains of The Thunderer, but it was too late. I was now in front of the judges who had watched our—my—humiliating show.

Afterward I sought the edge of the bus lot and crouched on a log until Mr. Girotta came and got me.

"I'm sorry!" I sobbed. He nodded and patted me on the shoulder. "Look, there's someone here," he said, producing Beanie.

"I couldn't see you!" Beanie said, in anguish. "I told Mr. G. I couldn't. I didn't hear the whistle, either. Those flanks took so long to go around—I had to wait for them, didn't I? I just couldn't leave those rows behind, could I? Then, I didn't know where you went, until you came running through!"

"Don't!" I put my face in my hands.

"You didn't even ride," Beanie said. "I've been looking for you."

"We lost," I said, crying.

"Yeah," he said, "I know we did. I guess we did it together." He lifted my hat from my lap. "Anyway, I was wondering. I mean after all this, would you—would you sit with me on the bus ride home?"

I turned to him in wonder. What did a trophy matter? Beanie liked me! I took his hand, and let him lead me back to the bus.

A Non-Catholic Upbringing

~~~~~~~~~~~~~~~~~~~~~

LEA CUNIBERTI-DURAN

Elementary School

I was born in Italy in the year 1967, just a year shy of the rising of the Student Movement and the other political movements that led to Europe's blood-stained 1970s. Italy, at the time, was very much a Catholic country; kids were named after saints, and prayers were taught in school.

I was born the odd kid out: my mother is Jewish but was raised Catholic, in an attempt to escape the brutality of World War II, and my father was a Catholic turned Atheist. It was decided that I would not be baptized. The official line was that I was "given more choices," and would be able to pick my religion as an adult.

In the mean time, my dad forbade me to go to church. I guess he did not want me to cloud my judgment or give in to peer pressure. Never mind that for the vast majority of people being part of a group is a sort of security blanket, and that for a kid, blending in is key.

Blending in for me was never very easy. For one thing, my name is Lea (can you find a name that's a bit more Jewish, please?). Then there were the facts that I was not baptized *and* didn't attend church.

I don't remember anybody giving me too much grief about not being baptized until I hit grade school. Enter Mrs. Renata Manzoni, the woman who was going to be my teacher for a very long four years. Mrs. Manzoni was one of those human beings who take it upon themselves to straighten out others. As an extremely devout Catholic, she could tell good from evil, and saving souls was high on her priority list.

It didn't take long for Mrs. Manzoni to find out that I was not Catholic, and at the beginning of the school year, she called me to the front of the class to introduce me to everyone: "Class, this is Lea. She is not baptized and she is going to Hell." Whispers spread across the class. Suddenly I was not viewed as just one of the other kids, but more like a newly discovered alien species.

The news spread quickly to the playground, and I immediately felt like a celebrity, but not the "She can jump double dutch" type—more the "Here comes the She-Devil" kind. It goes without saying that being six years old and pointed out as the Spawn of the Devil is no fun; although I felt that I was like everybody else, I was told that I was different.

I don't remember being teased because of my lost soul, but I do remember being shunned by some of the kids at school. One time I was having an argument with another kid, when we were interrupted by one of her friends who came to her rescue and shut me up by saying, "Don't talk to her, she's not even baptized." I remember feeling stunned, then livid, my ears red and burning. I watched their group as they walked away, gazing back at me, looking and then whispering and giggling.

Some other kids talked to their parents about my impending damnation; I guess that Mrs. Manzoni had struck a chord with some of my classmates. Some of those kids told me that I was not *actually* going to Hell; rather, I'd be in Limbo, where non-baptized, innocent souls spend eternity. To me, the Limbo deal seemed very much like a technicality, and not much of a consolation.

My parents, of course, reassured me that 'Hell' was just a form of social control enforced by the Church, so I ended up not worrying much.

As every major holiday and religious celebration came and went, I felt deeply alienated from the rest of my community. Although I attended a public school, we went to Mass as a class a few times each year. Many of the social and community activities rotated around the Church; it was the major catalyst. At a certain level not being able to participate made me almost not part of the community.

I felt very lonely; I was literally the only one I knew who was not at least baptized, even within my immediate family. If my parents had belonged to a different denomination, I could have at least known a few people with shared beliefs. Being the only one raised Atheist was something that forges one's personality in ways I am still discovering.

A few times I sneaked out behind my father's back (with my mother as an accomplice) and went to the after-church activities with the other kids. I really craved feeling, experiencing, and seeing what everybody else was doing on Sunday. I remember hearing all about the after-church programs on Monday at school, and to me, watching a movie, buying some candies, and hanging out while some of the older kids played foosball sounded nothing short of fantastic.

One time, I was invited by my friend Bruna to join her and her family after service. I was thrilled; it kept my mind occupied for several days. Finally Sunday came, and everything was just as I expected: a religious movie and the opportunity to buy liquorices and marshmallows. After the movie was over, we all exited the small room, which was outfitted with benches and an old projector. To my absolute horror, I spotted a priest who knew of me; I really could not escape his look of disapproval. He looked at me as though I had just stolen something. I felt so humiliated and ashamed.

When it was time for First Communion, it was clear that I was the only one in the entire school (read: in the entire country) who was going to skip the sacrament. I lived vicariously through the other girls, listening to their descriptions of their white dresses. Some of them would give me that look of "Ugh, what does she want?" if they realized I was eavesdropping. Others didn't say anything. I think they felt bad for me and didn't know quite what to say.

I stayed up late thinking about how it would feel to be part of what they were doing, to have that dress, to go to those rehearsals—to feel like I belonged. My best friend mercifully didn't talk about the whole thing, and tried not to make it too much of a big deal.

After the ceremony Mrs. Manzoni gave a gift and her teary-eyed congratulations to every child in the class.

Except for me, naturally.

A Misled Superhero

~~~~~~~~~~~~~~~~~~~~~

CINDY M. EMCH

Age ten at the time

In fifth grade, I finally started public school.

My mom was a public school teacher in our small farm town. I marched with her on the picket line when I was in second grade. But we didn't tell the other marchers that I was enrolled in the teeny tiny Catholic school in town. I was precocious, to put it kindly. I was super-geeky and couldn't get my head out of novels heavier than I was—that's another way to put it. After watching my brother get bored, antsy, and into trouble in our local public school, my mom decided to have me give our people, the Catholics, a shot.

I got a good education in books at Catholic school, but not in socializing. It was one of those places where when I arrived somehow everyone was already paired off. So I paired off with a book, and played with my neighborhood friends after school, fascinated by their stories of what sounded like paradise: The Public School.

After four grades of begging and pleading, my parents gave in for fifth grade. I got to go school shopping for clothes that weren't uniforms, and started Latson Road Elementary in Mr. Greate's fifth grade class. I felt so fancy and East Coast in my orange sweaters and brown jeans. I was a tiny fashionista after following my neighbors' clothing styles for all those years. I was beside myself with excitement. The trouble was, I was entering a complicated social structure with no handbook, and all of my public school pals were a couple of years older than me and so had already moved on to middle school.

On my first day I met two girls, Caroline and Daphne, who seemed friendly and nice. By nine in the morning we were the Three Musketeers. Total Best Friends. I was always a sucker for charming girls who could hold a conversation. I have always trusted easily. What I didn't yet know was that I was about to get a first-hand education about Best Friends.

When lunch came we ran around the yard, climbing and swinging and testing our daring by hanging upside down on the swings as we pushed each other higher and higher. Caroline said she'd be right back and skipped out of sight. Daphne and I didn't stop our dangerous swinging contest. We tried to see if we could twist the chains of our swings together to make the plastic and metal spin really fast and still flip upside down. It wasn't really working since we couldn't stop laughing long enough to wrap our legs around the chains once the swings separated.

Caroline ran back, out of breath and upset. "That boy! That boy! That boy is mean! He just pushed me!"

My breath stopped. Someone was being mean to my new best friend. This wasn't OK. This was what I heard about at home, when people talked about how men hurt women. This was sexism in action! This was like those men who were rude to my mom and talked to her like she was dumb! This was injustice! This was someone being a bully to my new best friend!

"Which one?" I asked her. I felt like my whole destiny rode on this. No one could pick on my new best friend when I liked to play football, my brother was a state champion wrestler, and my mom was a gym teacher! No one could challenge or hurt someone under my protection!

"Over there in the middle of the tire ring," she said. She looked upset and yet strangely proud. "What are you going to do?" she asked.

"Tell him that it's wrong to bully!" I said, and stomped away. I was full of a ten-year-old's righteous anger. I was going to Fight a Bully. I was going to Protect a Friend.

"Hey!" I yelled at a the culprit, a small fourth grader with sandy brown hair.

"Hi!" he said, smiling and waving at me.

"You shouldn't push girls," I said, grabbing his hand. "It's not right!" I said, louder and full of bluster. I pulled and swung on his arm, tossing him around in a curve.

"Hey, stop it! What are you doing? I didn't. I didn't push anyone!" he said.

He sounded so confused. I pulled him up and closer to me. "Don't lie to me. You pushed my friend. You're a bully!" I yelled. I started to slap him on the arms and back. Wherever my hands could reach, I was smacking him. He smacked back and tried to push me down.

"You're mean!" I shouted, palms still flying. He was crying and I was too mad to think. My head was fuzzy with anger, and cloudy with wondering how this had gotten out of control. I didn't want to be hurting this kid. And why did he look familiar? There were about twenty kids gathered around at this point as we pushed each other, him falling down and getting back up, both of us holding our ground.

"Stop it you kids! And on the first day of school!" Mrs. Elliot barked as she pulled us apart. There wasn't enough bad in either of us to fight a teacher.

A few minutes later we were sitting outside Principal Park's office. "Why did you start picking on me?" the boy asked.

Now that I wasn't Caroline's avenging angel, I recognized him. Jason, the kid brother of my brother's best friend. We had run in farm fields together. Gotten in hay bale fights and fed pigs together, laughing at their eagerness. He always let me brush the black horse because he knew it was my favorite chore. I felt so dumb. So ashamed.

"You pushed Caroline. The girl with the pink headband. You hurt her. I thought you were being a bully." I told him.

"But I didn't! She came over and kicked my ball away. I just chased after it."

I was so confused. The fight was over. I could tell he wasn't lying. Had I been completely duped by my new best friend? Had she just lied to see what would happen?

Principal Park called us in. He knew both of our families. I had known him as Greg ever since I could talk. He was always hanging out with my folks and saying "hi" when we were in town. "Cindy, you just started school here. I know you weren't a problem at St. Joseph's. Why did you beat up Jason?"

My superhero ego deflated. I couldn't explain to him how I was fighting for the good of the downtrodden, standing up to the bully hierarchy of the schoolyard, defending the rights of all poor little girls everywhere who got hurt, and trying to prove that girls weren't weak and made to be pushed around. It all rang so false now. I had been played. Manipulated. Tested. I was duped into being a self-righteous superhero for the amusement of a charming liar with a pink ribbon. "I thought he had bullied my friend. I was wrong. I am sorry."

Principal Park asked me about the bullying, and I told him what Caroline had told me, saying that I knew now that Jason hadn't done it. He still lectured Jason about bullying. He lectured us both about fighting. I defended Jason. Jason defended me. If I hadn't been crying so hard it would've been really funny. He called our parents, who were as confused as we were to hear that two friends who played together so well had just gotten into a legendary schoolyard fight.

When I walked back into class and took my seat in between Daphne and Caroline, I looked at Caroline accusingly. "Wow, I didn't think you'd start a fight. Why'd you do that?" she whispered. Her eyes sparked at me, daring me to get upset, daring me to call her out in the middle of class, interrupt Mr. Greate, and get in more trouble.

I swallowed something bitter. "I thought he was a bully."

My words sat there on the desk. I turned to the front of the room to hear the teacher. It was going to be a very different sort of school year.

The Joker's Wild

~~~~~~~~~~~~~~~~~~~~~

SHANNON DES ROCHES ROSA
Age nine at the time

By the time I got out of first grade, I had figured out that I must be special, because teachers always told me I was fantastic! and amazing! just because I was a good reader. This was like telling me I was good at breathing, because, duh, of course I was good at reading. It was my favorite thing to do. However, these adult reactions made me suspect that I had other super special secret talents that only certain adults could see, and, most importantly, that I didn't have to put any effort into.

Other kids didn't appreciate my specialness. I knew I was supposed to be interested in them, though, so I did silly things to make them pay attention to me. In second grade, I would curl up and pretend to cry near the big, hip, fifth grade girls, so that they would come over to coo and offer comfort. In third grade, I would chase boys around the playground, pin them down, and kiss them in front of a crowd of giggling girls who didn't have the nerve to give chase themselves.

I still didn't understand how to play with the other kids in any sort of natural way, but that was okay—they were rarely as interesting as my books, anyhow. In fact, most kids who did come over to play would, after about an hour, hunt down my mom and complain that they wanted to go home because I was ignoring them and sitting in my room, reading.

In fourth grade, my mom took me to try out for a kids' trivia television game show called The Joker's Wild. I thought it was a great idea; if I was on TV, then the other kids would have to acknowledge my supremacy!

My brothers coached me on television and cartoon trivia for the entire week before my audition: "What does Foghorn Leghorn always say?" "Where does Yogi Bear live?" Since I spent as much time in front of the tube as I did reading, the television-centric written screening was easy, and I qualified for the show. I was asked to come back for an interview with the staff.

I remember walking into a big office suite, and seeing an oval table surrounded by leather executive chairs, each one containing a person in a fancy suit. I had never seen people like them before, except, of course, on TV. But I knew that if any adults could sense my super special secret talents, it would be them.

The first question they asked me was, "What do you want to be when you grow up?"

My answer: "A singer!" (I didn't even know if I *could* sing, but I loved Olivia Newton John so very, very much.)

They then asked, "Can you sing for us right now?"

Me, aghast: "No!" (Couldn't they just sense that I would be a great singer?)

I was so embarrassed and perturbed by the failure of their specialness-detecting powers that I slumped under the table. Somehow I exited the room.

Somehow they never called me to be on the show.

And somehow the other kids at my school continued to ignore my secret specialness. But that was okay; I still had my books.

In fifth grade I hooked up with my missing pieces: Michael and Miho. They weren't interested in how I was special and different; they were interested in how much I was like them. Which was, to my surprise, the way to form an intense, volatile, yet wonderful friendship.

(And I would be remiss if I didn't add that the same Michael introduced me to my husband, and is my oldest child's godfather.)

Dodgeball Saves Lives

~~~~~~~~~~~~~~~~~~~~

JASON KOVACS

Age ten and eleven at the time

When I was nine years old my dad and I moved to a blue collar Seattle neighborhood called Ballard. We were always moving. The elementary school in Ballard, Benjamin Franklin Day Elementary, was just like the other five elementary schools I'd been to up to that point except that the building was kind of old. It had cloak rooms with banks of hooks at kid-level and a lot of dark wood trim. It had hardwood floors and big windows. The building was a holdover from the Roosevelt era and so were most of its teachers: old white guys in short-sleeved shirts and polyester slacks who sported thick glasses and bad tempers.

The most popular kid in my fourth grade class, my first class at B.F. Day, was John Hoffman. John was one of those kids who was just good at everything: good at sports, liked all the right music, always knew the answer, perfect handwriting, perfect grades, perfect hair. I didn't really have an opinion about John. There'd been one like him at every school

I'd attended and he was as expected, in his way, as the drinking fountain next to the bathrooms. I was busy being the new kid for the sixth time in three years and John was just another kid who didn't want to talk to me. His indifference was more welcome than the taunting of the bullies, but he never said two words to me and what I realized, at some instinctive level, was that whatever else John might have going for him, compassion wasn't on the list.

When the school year ended all us single-parent kids headed for our "off season" parents' places in far away lands and, when I came back the next year, I ended up getting moved to a mixed fifth and sixth grade class that was created three weeks into the school year. Kids were pulled from overcrowded classrooms to make the roster: two kids from each fifth grade class, two kids from each sixth grade class. And three weeks was long enough for teachers to decide who they didn't like, so I ended up in a class full of kids teachers hated.

It was kind of like The Breakfast Club meets The Dirty Dozen. We drove two teachers to quit in less than two weeks. We set one fire that resulted in the entire school being evacuated. And then we got Mr. Cash, a doctrinaire Jim Henson disciple and all-around cool guy. We made a tacit decision to keep Mr. Cash, and so my year progressed.

And while I hung out in my class full of reprobates and morons, John Hoffman was in some other class being perfect. Sometimes I'd see the light of his perfection bursting down the hall, like an explosion from an advanced placement chemistry class. He'd win the spelling bee, or publish an article in the Seattle Times Junior Journalist Program. The teachers talked about him in the hall. He was the superstar.

And me? I learned to make a bomb out of match heads that year.

The only place John and I had anything to do with each other was on the dodgeball court. B.F. Day had a dodgeball tradition that was unique in my public school experience: on the dodgeball court, kids tried to hurt each other. It wasn't just that we threw the balls as hard as we could, or aimed for each other's heads. I think all kids do that. But at B.F. Day we didn't use the standard red rubber dodge ball. At B.F. Day we used soccer balls, basketballs, and what I can only describe as pain balls: a kind of hard plastic ball that stayed spherical through rigidity rather than air pressure. B.F. Day dodgeball was all about the pain, and I was better at it than almost anyone, even John. However, in spite of my aptitude and my love of the game, I was away from the court the day someone broke John's leg with a soccer ball.

Of course I heard about it after the fact, but there wasn't much to the story: someone threw a soccer ball and it hit John in the knee. The whole joint went at once; the knee bent completely backwards and John went down screaming. We talked about it in hushed tones for the rest of the day and the principal said we couldn't play dodgeball with anything harder than a kickball from now on. There was some grousing about that but otherwise we were all just amazed that it was possible: how could you break someone's leg with a ball?

The kid who'd done it, Adam Mitchell, was the temporary superstar and undisputed badass of the court for five whole days. Even with kickballs, kids scattered out of the way of his throws like they were dodging freight trains.

John was out of school for a week before we heard that dodgeball had apparently saved his life. John had cancer and the tumor had weakened the bone in his knee. If it hadn't been for a fast-moving soccer ball, the doctors might not have found it in time and he could have died. He was going to lose his leg above the knee, but he would live, and it was dodgeball that had saved him. And this was another kind of notoriety for Adam Mitchell, but he still wasn't too happy about going back to getting picked last for team-ups.

When Mr. Cash related the story of John's knee to us, Gordy raised his hand.

"Yes, Gordy?"

"Does this mean we can play dodgeball with soccer balls again?" Gordy wanted to know.

And Mr. Cash said, "No."

After the initial cancer revelation, Mr. Cash gave us a little tutorial about what cancer is and why we never had to worry about catching anything from John. And while he was telling us this he also told us about chemotherapy and radiation therapy and said that John would lose his hair and get sick and lose weight. And the thing Mr. Cash kept emphasizing was that we all needed to support John. That he might feel weird and that we needed to let him know that he still had friends. And Mr. Cash didn't ever come out and say, "John's going to feel like a freak because he's gonna be bald and one-legged in a class full of healthy kids," but that was the message we took away. He gave us a phone number for the hospital and an address where we could send cards.

And I thought about that for the rest of the day.

And when I got home that night, I called John.

A kid picked up in the oncology ward—which I think might actually still have been called a cancer ward back then. I asked if John was there and the kid said yeah, hold on. There was some talking in the background. Then he came back and asked, "Who is it?"

"Jason," I said. "Jason Kovacs. From B.F. Day."

"Okay, hold on," said the kid.

More talking in the background. The kid came back.

"He's in the bathroom," the kid said.

"Oh," I said. "Okay. Should I hold?"

"If you want." I could hear the shrug through the phone.

"Um," I said. "Okay."

So he put the phone down and I spent a little while listening to kids talking and laughing in the background. Then the kid came back.

"You still here?" he asked.

"Yeah," I said.

"He's still in the bathroom. Chemo, you know."

"Yeah, okay," I said.

And he put the phone down. More talking and laughing in the background. Much longer wait. The kid picked up the phone again.

"You still there?" he asked.

"Yup," I said.

And I heard the distinctive sound of someone putting their hand over the receiver.

"Oh my God," said the kid. "He's still there!"

And then there was a lot of laughing.

The kid came on again a minute later and he almost had it together, but not quite.

"He's still in the bathroom," the kid said through a grin that distorted his words, even through the phone.

"Mmm-hmm," I said. "Okay. Thanks. Just. Uh. Tell him I called I guess."

"Sure thing," said the kid, and I could hear more laughter in the background; full on belly-laughing this time, and the kid was barely keeping his voice even.

And that was that.

I hung up the phone and stared at it for a while, thinking things over.

I tried it three more times later in the week, just to make sure I understood what was happening, and it was the same routine every time.

A few weeks later we heard that John had his surgery and everything went well. We heard he was doing wheelchair races in the halls and that the doctors were amazed at his progress. A month or two later he came back to school on crutches, with a fake aluminum leg.

The leg was on a catch, so John could make it fall off by pushing a button on his thigh. This was a big hit with the other kids and John was a superstar again in no time. As it happened, this was right about the same time Terry Fox, the famous one-legged cancer amputee, was making his epic run across Canada and so, of course, John started training for that right away and everyone knew he was going to make it.

As far as I know, he did.

He was still improving like a superhero two months into the next year, our sixth grade year, when a custody dispute took me out of town for four months. And by the time I got back to Seattle the school year was mostly over with.

I dropped out for my seventh grade year and my dad took me with him to Los Angeles.

I still think about John a lot.

I guess it's a good thing that he didn't ... I don't know—lower his standards to talk to a guy like me just because of a little cancer?

I don't know.

But that's the story of John Hoffman. Or at least, it's my version of it.

The Sex Change of Zyax II

~~~~~~~~~~~~~~~~~~~~

LIZ HENRY

Age ten at the time

Almost every day in fourth grade, my best friend Laurie Arminia and I would run outside to play under the geodesic dome monkey bars at recess. We'd comb through the sand with our fingers and explain to each other where everything was in our space city, and where the farms were, and the roads. I'd look up to see Laurie lost in thought with sand in her hands, her thick black hair flying around like a Shetland pony's mane. The gray steel monkey bar dome overhead saved our space colony people from the poison atmosphere of Planet Zyax, which we had named after a book called The Humans of Zyax II. Other people ran around whacking tether balls or playing four-square. Laurie and I were little kids. No one paid any attention to us. We'd climb to the top of the dome and survey our planet like twin gods. Twice a week, instead of going to recess, she and I would stay inside being "library aides," shelving books and helping kindergarteners learn to read. Doesn't it sound like a fairy tale too good to be true?

The next year everything changed, horribly. My family moved to Houston, Texas, which I had pictured as a sepia-toned dusty Western movie. Perhaps I'd ride my horse to school, tying it up to the hitching post!

That really was too good to be true. Texas was a brutal suburban landscape of malls and golf courses. The fifth grade girls wore three-inch heels. I was as short as most kindergarteners, still wore Garanimals, midget-sized Wranglers, and (horrors, for piano recitals) dresses with smocking across the chest. Middle class fifth grade Texas girls in 1980 wore Jordache jeans and couples-skated with boys at the roller rink. I was in deep trouble.

Luckily, before school started, I met Jennifer, who lived around the block. Though Jennifer was a year younger than me, she became my friend. I'd dial her phone number over and over; I can still hear the song of it in the beeps, 444-6784, 444-6784; a busy signal. Jennifer had a makeup mirror that flipped over and lit up to show what you looked like in night and day lighting, far away or magnified. She had enormous makeup kits. I'd lie on her waterbed (?!) to watch her smear on base, foundation, powder, eyeliner, lip liner, lipstick, mascara, and five kinds of eye shadow while we listened to Prince albums as loudly as possible and Jennifer insulted me in ways I didn't understand. "Quit watching me with your beady little roach eyes!" or "I think you're a Mexican, you have squinty eyes like a Mexican." It was as unlike Laurie Arminia as you could get. Jennifer was completely alien. I learned all the words to the Prince songs. Jennifer was like Prince, and David Bowie, with their makeup and thick eyeliner, screaming and posing, dancing on the rim of the bed, like all her gleaming album covers and posters and magazines.

One day at recess a horrible girl named Cheryl followed me outside from the "cafetorium." She had been making fun of how I ate my sandwich while reading a book. She wore suede ankle boots. Her mom's boyfriend took her and her mom on ski vacations. Cheryl said that reading was gay, and that I should be named Liz the Lez. To escape her, I went out into the blazing sun of the sidewalk and the heat-shimmering parking lot. Other kids followed us out, hooting. I saw Jennifer's face laughing at me in the crowd. She was chanting with them, "Liz the Lez, Liz the Lez." Someone pointed out that I was about to cry. People were crowding around me, too close, like stampeding animals. I felt sweaty and scared and a little dizzy. Sounds all started to blend together, babbling nonsense sounds, waves or wind or a waterfall over rocks.

Cheryl—with her blond, feathered hair and her disco metallic shirt—came right up into my face and said, "Is it true? I heard it was. I heard you used to be a boy, and you got a sex change. That's why you're so flat. You don't wear a bra. And you're like a boy and like boy things. Cause you're really a boy. *Lezzie*." I realized then that "Lez" meant lesbian. All the advice my mom and dad had ever given me to walk away and just ignore it flew out of my head. I felt like my body disappeared, and I became a cloud of light and air. And I said, in a voice that could rule the world:

"That's the dumbest thing I've ever heard in my entire life! How could I have a sex change when I'm only in fifth grade? I haven't even hit puberty yet! And even if I had a sex change, so what if I did? And if I was a boy, I wouldn't be a lesbian, don't you know anything? And we're little kids, you dumbass, we don't have sex anyway, which is what it means, it's about who you have sex with, I have read about it, and people have the right to do whatever they want because it's a free country, and I believe in free love and I have constitutional rights, and I'm not a lesbian, I'm bisexual!"

Then my body came back into sweaty existence, and my head came back down onto my body, and I ran into the school and hid in the bathroom and cried so hard that snot ran down the back of my throat and I sort of choked and threw up. I went to the nurse, and my mom came to get me. When they asked me what happened, I just said that I threw up after lunch. I spent the rest of the day in bed with an ice-cold towel on my head, sipping ginger ale, reading science fiction, and feeling very confused.

I was still friends with Jennifer until ninth grade. My mom said that Jennifer was a bad person to be friends with, that she wasn't nice. My mom was right, but there was something my mom didn't get. I needed to understand what Jennifer's deal was.

My life has been something of a variation on that theme ever since.

Khaki

~~~~~~~~~~~~~~~~~~~~~

MEREDITH LOM

Age six to age twelve

When I was little, one girl in my grade school class was the boss of all the other little girls. There was nothing special about her, really, save for being the youngest daughter in a big Mormon family; but in my town, even that wasn't exceptional.

Her parents had even given her the most boring name in the book—they'd named her Khaki. She was one of those impossibly tiny creatures whose hair and skin were all the same translucent color. She was the pied piper of the playground, and since all the little girls had "friend crushes" on her, she could always get them to do her bidding.

One time, I invited her over to play on a Saturday, and she accepted, and the parental dance was done, and she came over to my house. She and her mother pulled up in their yellow convertible (which was roughly the same color as her hair and skin). They found me playing in the yard. I was probably a mess like I was most Saturdays, being something of a tomboy. My father, then a dark-haired thirty-something with a preference for short red running shorts with white piping (which, come to think of it, were actually in fashion at that point), had been cursing and sweating and clipping the lawn.

Khaki and her mother took one look at the mess of us out there and climbed back into their hideous car. Her mother said, loudly, "Come along, Khaki, we don't play with these kind of people." And they left.

For the rest of grade school, Khaki was the master of my social demise—of my not getting invited to birthday parties, of my not being included, of my not being asked to wear the same outfit as the other little girls on the same day. Khaki was vicious. The little girls would all do musicals together, under Khaki's direction, and I would not be included. I would watch, in quiet horror, as she distributed invitations to her parties, events, and shows—and deliberately skipped my desk. I was paralyzed by the exclusion.

I would say to the teacher, "Don't you think it's unfair that she doesn't invite everyone?" And year after year, the teachers would look at me blankly, as if to tell me that unfairness was just part of growing up. Maybe that was true, and it was a painful lesson that we all had to learn. But that didn't make it any easier when Khaki passed my desk after handing out candy hearts to the rest of the class. She would smile at me as she passed, polite as ever, but never once stopped to place a Valentine in my heart-shaped holiday folder. Being left out of her circle was heartbreaking.

Khaki's family moved to Utah during the summer before sixth grade. The other little girls threw her a lavish going-away party at someone's backyard pool. They handed out invitations on the last day of fifth grade. By that time, our public school had instituted a rule that if students were going to distribute invitations in the classroom, they would have to invite the whole class. So the girls handed out the coveted envelopes on the playground. I was grateful that I didn't get one. I had never been quite so relieved to see someone go away.

Years later, after I'd forgotten about Khaki entirely, I bumped into her in Los Angeles, by chance. I was a college student, and she was working at the local convenience store. "My parents said I could come out here for a year and try to make it as a backup dancer!" she exclaimed, happy to see me. But seeing her made me feel like I had been cheated. I had expected her to go on and do something fabulous and breathtaking. I had expected her to be the boss of all of Los Angeles. In reality, she was a store clerk, just trying to make a living.

She was tall, no longer impossibly tiny, and her hair was no longer yellow, rather a colorless gray. She had bumpy red skin, a bad haircut, and a round face. She was not an attractive grownup. I smiled and nodded, and paid for my granola bars and cheese. Then I ran back to my dorm room to join my friends for a party. Khaki was not invited.

Lisp

~~~~~~~~~~~~~~~~~~~~~

ARUNI WIJESINGHE-LEWIS
Elementary School

Every other Thursday afternoon
The year I am in third grade
William O. Schaeffer Elementary
I go to speech therapy to have my lisp corrected

Small cinderblock room no bigger than a closet
Across the hall from the library
Wendy, Andrew Mallon, and I meet with the school speech therapist
A middle-aged woman with thick calves and
Perfect elocution
We spend forty minutes reciting words
Full of serpentine "s" sounds
Brows knitted in concentration above pursed child-mouths
Soft susurration accompanies the sound of
Rubber-soled Keds squeaking against industrial gray linoleum

Brightly colored placards glare down at us
Cartoon mouths grimace
Illustrate the proper shapes of vowels
Bite off bits of consonants

The speech therapist is well intentioned
She wills my unruly tongue to repent
Coaxes unwilling s's from behind
Bared baby teeth

She never realizes
She has been mispronouncing my name
      since the beginning of the school year
Elongating vowels, misplacing accents
Anglifying the music of my ancient Sanskrit name

I am too ashamed to correct her.

The Survey

~~~~~~~~~~~~~~~~~~~~~~~~

ALISON WEISS

Age twelve at the time

It's 1975 in Southern California, and I have entered junior high. "Love Will Keep Us Together" blasts from every car stereo, and it never really gets cold enough to wear a coat. I begin to understand what the Beach Boys meant by "endless summer," even though I'm not the kind of beach babe the Beach Boys sing about. At age twelve, I'm thin with pale skin, straight black hair, and wire-framed glasses that are perpetually bent and sliding down my nose.

My family and I have landed in this beach town after stunning bad luck. My parents' dream to run an alcoholism treatment center has failed utterly after less than a year. In short order, they have lost everything they own and are living in a rental house with me and my four sisters. My father is gone every weekend to make money. My mother works full time as a nurse in a psychiatric hospital. During our first six weeks in Los Angeles, my youngest sister gets hit by a car and spends all summer in a body cast and then a wheelchair.

There is no money for clothes. My grandmother has learned to sew and specializes in quick-and-easy polyester. Each girl is given a huge bag of my grandmother's creations. I start seventh grade in a powder-blue polyester pantsuit. People ask me so many times that first day who made my outfit that by the time the last bell rings, I've taken to lying that I bought it at Orbach's department store.

It's hard enough to learn to navigate through Oceanview Junior High's long halls, but I'm doing it alone. I want something that is out of my reach: a friend. Not a group of friends—that's way beyond hope—but I'll take a friend. It doesn't even have to be a best friend, just a friend to save me a seat in class. I can't impress people with my athletic skills because I'm terrible at sports, and I'm already out of the fashion race because of my homemade wardrobe. The only thing I think I have going for me is that I'm smart. So, I do the unthinkable—I actually show my intelligence. I write ten-page reports for science class. In English, the teacher chooses my poem to read aloud. For a while, my academic success carries me—and then it takes me straight to Hell.

It starts out as an ordinary day. In social studies, I raise my hand too often, answering a question correctly that Christy got wrong—Christy, who is the leader of a gaggle of girls, and who doesn't like to be embarrassed. She gets perky, sporty Jax, her second lieutenant, to take me down. Without catching the attention of our teacher (who has tired hair and always reeks of cigarettes), Jax starts passing around a note, some kind of survey. It makes its surreptitious way around the classroom, and there is lots of giggling. It doesn't reach me before the bell rings.

The next period is math. I slide into my seat, and Jax walks by, casually slipping the survey onto my desk. It's my turn, I think, to see what everyone was laughing about. There is only one question on the survey: Who thinks Alison is a geek? My eyes slide down the paper, and I see that all my classmates have signed it with cruel embellishments. "She's the geekiest." "She stinks." "She's greasy." My stomach drops and I almost stop breathing. I dig my nails into my palms to stop from crying, but it doesn't work. I have never felt more alone. There is not one safe person in the room.

And the worst part of this story? I will keep that survey rolled up in my nightstand drawer to take out and re-read. I will not lose my sense of utter loneliness for years.

Fish Face

~~~~~~~~~~~~~~~~~~~~~~

ELSWHERE

Age thirteen at the time

I was a nerd in junior high school, but my friend A. was even worse off. She was new in town, she wore weird clothes, and her family didn't have any money. She looked funny, too; all the kids called her "Fish Face."

In spite of these strikes against her, A. was mysteriously self-confident. In eighth grade, she decided to run for student council vice president. I was aghast: everyone knew student council was just a popularity contest, and A. was anything but popular. What was she thinking?

But A. didn't seem worried. She made posters, campaigned, did everything a student council candidate was supposed to do. Just as if she had a chance.

On the morning of the election, the whole school gathered in the auditorium to hear the candidates' speeches. One after another, the candidates for treasurer and secretary stood at the podium and read carefully rehearsed banalities about how they would dedicate themselves to improving the school.

Finally, it was A.'s turn. My stomach clenched. I was mortified for her already. She was sure to say something weird, and even if she didn't, just her being who she was and standing up in front of everyone was sure to be social suicide. It was bad enough that she got teased and harassed in the halls and at lunch: how much worse could it be to see her humiliate herself in front of the entire school?

A. stood up and approached the podium. The room rang out with hoots and whistles and cries of "Fish Face!" until the principal made everyone be quiet. A. waited patiently for silence, then began her to read her speech.

"Some of you call me Fish Face," she said.

Pandemonium erupted! Once again the principal called for silence. When it was quiet enough for her to be heard, A. calmly continued her speech. She talked about how regardless of names people called her, the important thing was whether or not she would get things done on the student council. She talked about changes that needed to be made, and about her ideas for making them. She talked about how everyone said that student council was just a popularity contest, but that this was our chance to prove them wrong.

Everywhere in the halls that day, you heard the words, "Fish Face." Fish Face! Nobody could believe it. Nobody could believe she'd had the nerve. Nobody could stop talking about it.

A. won the election.

The Real Meaning of Might

~~~~~~~~~~~~~~~~~~~~~~~~

AMANDA JONES

Age eight at the time

I had a pedestrian, mildly tortured school experience, learning to sort between what mattered and what didn't, with only the typical betrayals and embarrassments. It was my brother who suffered the brunt of the pre-teen flailing, and watching what he went through taught me more than all the bullying I endured.

Marco was (and still is) my sweet older brother. As a child he was scrawny, friendly, funny, affectionate, and energetic. And he had Williams Syndrome, which meant he was a special needs kid. Only in those days no one had yet thought up political correctness, so my brother was just "retarded."

Williams Syndrome is a genetic disorder with a long, scary list of symptoms. When I look up the most common of them, it says: "Unusual facial structure, developmental retardation, short stature, heart problems, and puffiness around the eyes. Personality traits include being overtly friendly, trusting strangers, and an affinity for music." My brother had all of these traits. He still does.

For most of elementary school, other children were kind to Marco. They included him in games and they'd even willingly invite him to their birthday parties. But at age twelve, this swiftly changed. As hormones began their insidious creep, kids who were once friends became blatantly cruel.

My brother and I did not go to school together. He went to an all-boys school, and I went to an all-girls. But we lived opposite a park and would go there together almost daily. I was three years younger. He was my only sibling, my big brother, my friend, and often my rival and archenemy. I loved him. I didn't know to be embarrassed of him, even when he laughed inappropriately loudly or let fly with the animal noises he was prone to making when overexcited. But as he got older, he would embarrass the other kids, as if just knowing him made them uncool.

One awful day my mother was called to my brother's school. She brought Marco home with red eyes that were even puffier than usual. Two former friends had cornered him and beaten him up in the bathroom, calling him Mongol, circus freak, animal. He could not understand what had happened, and his face registered only confusion and disorientation. And for the first time in my life I felt real, adult rage. It sped through me like fire, closing my throat and making me break out in a sweat. I was eight years old and had just felt the shock of injustice.

Marco stayed home for a week to recover. There were hushed phone calls with the low hum of my mother's fury venting into the mouthpiece. Marco and I lived alone with our mother. Our father had hit the road with a younger woman when I was five. He couldn't handle raising a "retard." At the time I didn't think much about what it must have taken for my mother to raise the two of us alone for so many years. Now I do, and I am staggered.

A month after the incident, Marco and I encountered the perpetrators at our park. My brother flinched when he saw them, his "overt friendliness" damaged. He wanted to go home. He started making noises. His hands came up over his head. The boys, angry that the "retard" had caused them innumerable hours of detention, strode towards him, fists balling, mouths ugly grimaces. At first fear turned my legs and stomach soft. And then, in a sort of miraculous intervention, the rage hit me again and I became possessed. I raced towards the boys yelling words that had never dared cross my lips before.

"You bastards!" (I'd heard my mother call my absent father that often and suspected it was a terrible slight.)

"You stupid, mean little bastards. You assholes! You keep away from my brother!"

And my God, it worked. It actually worked. The boys didn't know what to do next. They stopped, their faces froze and they stood there looking just like stupid little assholes.

The best part of all is that my brother started to laugh. He laughed his inappropriately loud laugh with a few animal noises thrown in for good measure. The boys sloped off, vanquished, with that sound at their backs. It was wonderful. Admittedly I was an eight-year-old girl and even mean boys probably knew better than to beat up a small female child, but it was the first genuinely empowering moment of my life. And I guess I learned that it was actually possible to stand up against injustice.

Many years later, I used my brother shamelessly as an acid test for the men I dated. If they were embarrassed of my brother or they were mean or ignored him (and most did), they didn't last long. They were filed in the Stupid Asshole category and dispatched. And then I met a guy who was different. He didn't deal with Marco like he was retarded. He wasn't overly condescending or patronizing or even sickly solicitous. He treated him like an adult who liked to laugh loudly, hug people, and dance erratically. He called him Big Man, which made Marco's skeletal chest swell with pride. Greg was doing an MBA at an elite business school filled with future captains of industry who wore button-down shirts. One night, he invited Marco and me to a party with his fellow students. I was edgy, thinking that my brother's unbridled enthusiasm for singing and dancing, or even the animal noises, might cause a scene, and I really liked Greg and didn't want to have to dispatch him quite so quickly.

When we got there, Greg casually took Marco around, introducing him not as his girlfriend's brother, but as his "buddy." He gave Marco a beer and let him loose. Hours later, from across the room, I noticed a circle forming on the dance floor. With rising dread, I broke through the crowd to face what was happening. Marco and Greg were both lying on their backs, spinning in circles, breakdancing to "Red, Red Wine" by UB40. The crowd cheered and clapped and my brother hooted and glowed. Marco had found a hero, and I had found a husband.

The Sound of Musicals

~~~~~~~~~~~~~~~~~~~~~~

MICHAEL PROCOPIO

Age six to the present

The men in my family loved show tunes. My grandfather, being of Italian stock, listened to opera. My father preferred Broadway musicals. Original cast albums like Cinderella, Camelot, A Chorus Line, and Annie followed us wherever we traveled in his car. My older brother loved big movie musicals, specifically those produced by Arthur Freed and his friends at Metro Goldwyn Mayer Studios. Most directly influenced by my brother, since I spent the most time under his watchful eyes, I learned to converse in a language liberally peppered with musical references. We compared the events of our own lives to those in the movies, usually unfavorably, since it is often difficult to make homework and cleaning up after dogs more interesting than dancing around on pirate ships or singing with Munchkins.

The women in my family, however, were not consumed by show tune mania. Instead, they fixed things. My mother, who never seemed to listen to much of anything, fixed dinner. My clarinet-playing sister, who preferred music performed by men in very tight trousers, fixed computers. My grandmother, whose only hint at musicality was the incessant whistling of "Tumbling Tumbleweeds," often threatened to "fix my wagon," but never followed through.

In my family, a boy singing songs from The Sound of Music was nothing extraordinary—in fact, it was encouraged. The subtle changing of lyrics to suit any occasion was applauded by my elder brother. Sadly, singing "I Am Six, Going on Seven" in a voice approximating that of the eldest Von Trapp girl did not translate well to the playground of my elementary school. Worse, my impression of Ann-Margret's frenzied "Smash the Mirror" number from Tommy was not received with applause but with baffled silence, then derisive laughter, which I found confusing since my brother and sister had both loved the impression as I performed it the day before. Upon review some thirty years later, it seems reasonable that a six-year-old boy writhing on the on the grass and pulling at his hair while singing in an exaggerated vibrato might make other little boys uncomfortable. It was clear to them that I was different. It was clear to me that they simply did not speak my language.

By the second grade, my performances were much more subtle, intended for more intimate audiences. To offset the boredom of a long bus ride to Olvera Street in Los Angeles, I decided to entertain my field trip seatmate, whom I thought looked rather like a juvenile Gene Kelly, with a song. I had chosen to sing "Take Me Out to the Ballgame" to him, which was the most boy-friendly song I knew. I had hoped he might appreciate my cleverness in selecting the title song of a film made by an actor who looked like him. He did not. Neither did he appreciate the fact that I chose to sing it like Esther Williams rather than Frank Sinatra or

Jules Munshin. Far from being entertained, he squirmed, and moved as far away as he could from me without hurling himself from the bus. I thought he'd understand. I don't think he spoke to me again until the third grade. I rode the rest of the way to Los Angeles in silence; my status as a resident alien confirmed.

There were few opportunities to further humiliate myself since I did not sit with other boys at lunch, get invited to their houses, or even play with them unless compelled to in group sports like dodgeball, wherein they sharpened their throwing skills and I perfected my dodging abilities.

If a boy admits to liking show tunes, he invites trouble. If a boy who likes show tunes also admits to dreaming about taking bubble baths with Michael Landon, he invites danger. To my mind, liking musicals seemed a perfectly normal, masculine thing to do. Blowing kisses to the shadow in the shape of Mr. Landon cast by my night-light every evening did not. I'd never heard of another boy doing that, so I kept my mouth shut, which felt unnecessary, since everyone seemed to know anyway.

Names like "girl" and "sissy" were first muttered and then shouted at me. As we got a little older, the words "fag" and "homo" entered the vocabulary. I objected to "girl" since I had no desire to be one, Ann-Margret impression aside. "Sissy" I wasn't so sure about—I was bigger and faster than most of my taunters, but I was mildly obsessed with people like Charo and activities such as watching Days of Our Lives. By the time fifth grade came and the abandoned fantasies of Michael Landon were replaced by thoughts of holding hands with a tall Brazilian-Swedish boy, I knew my taunters were speaking the truth when they called me a homo; but I also knew that they did not mean it as a compliment.

The name-calling eventually led to physical threats. The occasional sock in the arm or leg stuck out to trip graduated to stomach punching and being shoved against walls. Once, cornered in the library by one of the meanest boys I knew, I implored him to leave me alone and reminded him of the nearby presence of our school librarian. He laughed as cruelly as a nine-year-old could without descending into parody and suggested I go run and cry to her as he punched me hard in the stomach. I ruled out the use of successful reasoning as I doubled over, the air escaping from my lungs. A quick inventory of other options made me decide that the best course of action was to bury my fist as far as possible into his eye socket. He screamed, cried, and ran—everything he had predicted I would do. I stood there among the stacks of books stunned by my act of retaliatory violence and shocked at the condition of my hand—it hurt like hell. That never seemed to happen to people in the movies.

The following year, the boy was placed in a classroom for children with learning disabilities. I dismissed the thought that I had caused his brain damage as I admired his new eyeglasses from a very safe distance. At least, I thought, he wouldn't be bothering me again. For the most part, no one else did either.

The rest of my elementary school career was spent trying to be as un-unsettling to others as possible. When forced to play soccer with my classmates, my attention would often turn away from the ball and to the nearby boundary fence covered in honeysuckle vines. When the vines were in bloom, the class would break from play to swarm the flowers. It was one mild mania I could share with the others, at least. I sometimes quietly hummed Lena Horne's Honeysuckle Rose from Thousands Cheer as I sucked the nectar from the blossoms. Quietly, because I knew the penalties for sharing with my classmates the fact that I had a song for nearly every occasion. Of course, my brother would understand. I'd tell him, since he was the only person in my life who spoke Musical better than I did and I knew he would have done the same thing, since he was rather hopeless at team sports himself. As long as I had him to talk to when I got home from school, I remained relatively untroubled by my scholastic isolation.

Then, in my twelfth year, three major events occurred that altered the course of my social life: I started middle school, entered into an aggressive attack of puberty, and my brother moved to France, where he could watch musicals in French, thus combining two of his greatest passions. Though the news he sent of Gene Kelly dancing and singing with Catherine Deneuve in Les Demoiselles de Rochefort made me nearly faint from excitement, our conversations were few, given the physical distance between us. The combination of being in a new school environment with a rapidly changing body and no brother to confide in made the issue of my own social awkwardness more acute. Since my body and voice had decided to change without first consulting me, I decided I might as well change my personality, too. Twelve-year-olds are like that.

I watched the other puberty-stricken people around me, noting what they wore and what they listened to and, eventually, how to be more like them, to blend in. Never entirely, but enough to be accepted, invited to parties, and allowed to sit with others at lunch. Instead of humming

Rodgers and Hart tunes in public, I started tapping my feet to Hall and Oates, the Go-Go's, and other musicians favored by 'tweens in 1982. I learned to speak the language of the people around me, to enter their world and erase some of my former reputation as an alien. I succeeded to some degree, gaining friends and higher social status—but I always felt it was an act, and not one involving giant revolving wedding cakes or disembodied arms playing an orchestra full of instruments, as I would have secretly preferred. On the outside, I could appear as normal as most other boys, barring a few minor quirks like apple seed necklaces. Inwardly, I knew I was a fraud, but I was so relieved to walk among them without having insults or more tangible objects thrown at me that I vowed never to let the name Judy Garland pass my lips again. In public.

As I got older and entered college, I found what I had secretly given up hope of ever finding—people my age who spoke openly of Leslie Caron, Alice Faye, and Donald O'Connor. People who spoke my language. People like me. And they didn't look like aliens, but rather like attractive human beings who were proud of being different from ninety percent of the population. Eventually, I learned to look upon my show tune-loving tendencies as a source of pride.

Now, I sometimes sing out loud specifically to annoy people. In fact, if you happen to walk through my neighborhood and you listen very carefully, you might hear a bit of Mary Poppins or Meet Me in St. Louis coming from the open window of my apartment as I sing right along. And I don't really care who hears me.

All's Fair in Love and Mucus

~~~~~~~~~~~~~~~~~~~~~~

SJ ALEXANDER

Age twelve at the time

I grew up in a small town outside of Chicago where the summers were so hot it felt like your skin was about to melt off and you suspected you would be cooler that way, and the winters were so cold your freshly-washed hair would freeze solid at the bus stop.

This was the end of the eighties, during the last gasp of the big poodle hair craze. In the eighth grade I had my crazy tangle out front teased up until it could ensnare low-flying bats. I was so proud of it! This, combined with my tendency to carelessly leave the house with the back of my head still wet, combined with my gigantic hoop earrings that could double as belts in a pinch, meant I wasn't one to wear a woolly hat. So, I was sick all the time, all winter long, and I tend to think that there was a relationship between my constant sickness and my habits.

Despite being smart overall (other than the hat thing), I was in Math Facts for Complete Morons that year, which felt like torture to me. There was not a bone in my body or a dusty, forgotten corner of my brain that could make me retain math, I'm sorry to say. Even in college when I was required to take algebra and I did every extra assignment, studied hard, and got help from the teacher, I barely squeaked by with a B. Currently I'm pretty good with practical math, such as grocery store deals and restaurant tipping, but I was hopeless in those days. So there I was for the 4,000th time, studying basic math facts.

Fact: I was deeply, deeply bored.

Fortunately, I had something else to focus on: I was completely in love with the boy who sat across the room from me. I could stare at him for the whole hour, because our desks were broken up into two groups of rows that faced each other, with a big aisle down the middle. I was almost right across from him, but one row over, so lucky for me no one was blocking the view of his utter handsomeness.

Rather than fussing with fractions, I studied this boy. I noticed how many times in a week he wore his favorite sweater (orange with a snowflake pattern) and if he had gotten his hair cut (bowl cut to shorter bowl cut). Once he was out sick for three days, leaving me alone to twist and fidget in my seat as if I was being burned at the math stake.

Yearly, usually in January, the whole school would be hit by that coughy-phlegmy plague that lingers for weeks. I had an unsympathetic mother who would only let me stay home if there was solid evidence I was bleeding from a major artery, or nonstop rocket-style vomiting. So there I was in my math class, at that stage of a cold where you feel the need to sneeze constantly.

Fact: School girls find normal bodily functions embarrassing.

The whole class was sitting quietly, working on some math problems. I had the most tortuous tickle—it was as if the entire contents of my head were trying to escape. If only I was at home and could sneeze and blow until I felt better, but no. If I did that in class it would mean my classmates would know I was human, and did disgusting things like sneeze. If I couldn't even sneeze, then nose-blowing was absolutely out of the question.

I kept holding my sneezes in, making pathetic little "Eep! Eep!" noises, feeling more and more as if my head would pop. I would not be caught dead carrying something as practical and grandma-like as tissues, so even as I began to wish I had some, I continued suffering in squeaky near-silence. Some people, bored to death with their basic math facts, leaned over to whisper, "Bless you." My math teacher had even thoughtfully provided a box of tissues on the corner of his desk for student use, but there was no way I was going to parade across the room in front of the boy I liked and fire up the schnozz trumpet.

Desperately, I began to consider my options. Could I make it up to the front and whisper for permission to go to the bathroom? I didn't think so. My eyes were so watery that the math problems on the paper in front of me were beginning to blur and swim. I was going to ... oh, no.

Fact: I was totally hosed.

"WHAA-CHOOOOO!" I lost it, breaking the heavy mathy silence that blanketed the classroom. I clapped my hand, covered with the too-long sleeve of my sweatshirt, over an upper lip, mouth, and chin that were all now densely covered with a shiny snot goatee.

I froze where I was, and glanced around furtively. A couple more people tossed a "Bless you" my way. No one seemed to be paying attention. Even the teacher was busy marking our pop quizzes from that morning. With trepidation, I looked across the room. There was the object of my secret love, brows knitted, working away at his math problem. Whew. Sleeve still in place, I hunched down over my work and tried to figure out what to do next, as my face burned. At least I could see my paper again.

I scraped off a little bit of the snot goatee at a time. I still think it was probably the most fluid that has ever come out of my head. Could I hide under my hands and ask for permission to go to the bathroom now? No. It would be even more embarrassing now that my face had exploded. I kept working away at the snot, a little bit at a time. To my horror and deepening panic, the part of the sleeve I was working on became totally saturated and I had to roll the snot up inside my sleeve. I turned to the other sleeve, lamenting the fact that it was my favorite sweatshirt (I thought it was hilarious: "I think, therefore, I party," plus it was big, warm, and comfortable). Would this ruin it? I kept glancing over at my crush, who, as usual, did not notice I existed.

Finally, my face was dry and my sleeves were rolled up to my elbows. I was saved! I touched my face repeatedly to make sure I was clean. I congratulated myself on my cleverness.

Then, my crush nonchalantly slid his chair back and stood up from his desk. He strolled across the room, took a tissue out of the box, and quietly blew his nose with his back to the class.

Oh, *disgusting*. How could he get up and blow his nose in front of the whole room? It was at that moment that I noticed he had a funny-shaped head and ... was that a boil next to his nose? I, the girl with her own snot ensconced inside not one but both sleeves, discovered that I did not love this boy as much as I thought. Love is fickle that way, I guess.

Spitting Image

~~~~~~~~~~~~~~~~~~~~~~

JOHN H. KIM

Age ten at the time

Fifth grade was a low point in my life. I had finally made some friends in third grade, and gotten through fourth. Then we moved to the other side of the mountain, to a huge, run-down old house overlooking the Hudson River. My parents had bought it as a fixer-upper, and I think got a real deal. It had a four-and-a-half acre mostly wooded lot, with a garage that used to be an old stable. There were no other houses for quite a distance, which made it kind of lonely.

We lived off highway 9W instead of a regular street, so the school bus didn't stop near our house. I walked to school instead, which was only a quarter-mile if I cut through our enormous mountain lot to the dead end of Franklin Street. This involved trekking over a wide grassy path through the woods, past an old swimming pool. The walk was bearable some days, but when I had orchestra practice and had to lug my French horn, it was a real pain.

I had a hard time adjusting to the new school. I missed my friends Mark and Jason, and would call them on the phone a lot. At some point into the school year I finally invited someone from orchestra over to our house. I can't remember his name anymore. I remember he played a woodwind of some sort, certainly something a lot lighter to lug to my house than a French horn.

When he came over, my mother was home. She brought us some snacks, then we looked through my stuff and around the house. We didn't talk about anything in particular, and didn't play games like I did with my old friends. Then we went outside to the big yard. The garden was still probably a mess, but it was big. Suddenly, he got mad over something, and yelled, "The problem with you is that you think you're the spitting image of your mother!" Then he stalked off.

I had absolutely no idea what he was talking about.

I couldn't recall exactly what we had been talking over, but it didn't seem to involve my mother. I cast my mind in all directions, trying to think what it could mean. Was it some sort of clever dig at my looks? I hated clever insults, or rather I hated being embarrassed for not understanding them. Was it a play on words, something about "spitting"? Insults often seem to invoke mothers.

Then something occurred to me. My mother was white, and my father was Korean. Did that have something to do with it? I still didn't understand why he said that, but it did seem to make a sort of sense. In fact, I realized he was right. I didn't think of myself as Korean at all. I didn't interact with my father much, so most of my mannerisms came from my mother.

Still, it was a puzzle. My visitor was white, but I think he was from an immigrant family of some sort, maybe Eastern European. What would make him say that? I couldn't remember what would prompt that, but then, I didn't remember much about what we talked about anyway. As far as I can remember, we didn't talk or hang out after that for the rest of the year. I certainly never asked him what he meant by it, or what made him say it.

It did make me think about a lot of things. I still remembered some of the popular chants from elementary school. One was "Chinese; Japanese; Dirty knees; Look at these!" done pushing up and down your eyebrows, then pulling out your shirt like breasts. I didn't understand what was behind those rhymes as I thought about what he had said, but I somehow knew they were related.

I made it through the rest of the year at that middle school, but I never made any friends. The next year, my parents put me in a private prep school across the river. It was a long bus ride, but the bus would stop at our house. Some things changed, but others didn't. I still didn't think of myself as Korean for the most part, but sometimes I would stop and think about the incident, and my image.

From the Bleachers

~~~~~~~~~~~~~~~~~~~~~

ELS KUSHNER

Age thirteen at the time

In seventh grade, I got a crush on my French teacher. A huge, yearning, painful crush. On my female French teacher. It hit me like a truck, and it was terrifying. Particularly so because I read a lot and knew exactly what it was called if these sorts of feelings for people of the same gender continued; I had it on good authority that they could be "just a phase," and I hoped fervently that they were.

See, all those advice books for adolescents—the ones with questions supposedly from real teens about things like menstruation and pubic hair—always included a question from some poor soul along the lines of "I think I have a crush on my best friend, s/he's a girl/boy and so am I, does this mean I'm gay?" To which the answer was always something like, "Now, there's absolutely nothing wrong with being gay. But *don't worry* [emphasis mine] about your crush on your friend; it's perfectly normal for heterosexual teens to have feelings like this..." and blah blah blah. It was supposed to be reassuring but was actually confusing: if there was nothing wrong with being gay, what was there to worry about, with the crushes on friends? Why the need for reassurance? Anyone would smell a rat.

In seventh grade, I tried to put the whole emotional mess behind me and concerned myself with the standard teenage girl nerd things: reading the Foundation Trilogy, writing in my notebook, and trying not to get beat up by mean kids.

The mean kids were really, really mean. Especially Noelle Johnson, who was constantly threatening to beat me up because I was so bad at volleyball. Noelle was one of those girls who were mysteriously allowed to spend every gym class sitting on the bleachers, gossiping and making obnoxious comments. (And you have to wonder: why did she care about me? I wasn't even on her team!)

One day Noelle ventured down from the bleachers again. I figured she was going to give me yet another hard time about how my inability to spike the ball was going to lead to my imminent demise at her hands. Instead, she stared at me, hard, and demanded accusingly, "Are you a lesbian?"

My jaw dropped. My first impulse—honestly, I was this nerdy—was to say something like, "How am I supposed to know if I'm a lesbian? I'm only thirteen! No one can know if they're a lesbian when they're thirteen! All the books say so! I'm waiting to see. Ask me again in a few years." But even I knew that that would've been a big mistake. Though, in retrospect, maybe not worse than what I did say, which was (after a few seconds during which all the above thoughts flashed through my mind) a bare and unconvincing "No!"

As it was, she stared at me for a couple more seconds, while all her friends said "OooOOoooh!" with the rising inflection that indicates a fight is about to start. But nothing happened. She made a few more remarks about how dumb I was and went back to the bleachers.

I went back to the volleyball game, shaken. How had she known to ask? How?

Now I think that she probably just randomly picked the most damning accusation she could come up with. But at the time it was so scary and creepy, like she could see inside my thoughts. If she could do that when I wasn't even sure how I felt, what would happen if I decided that I really was gay? It was too terrible to contemplate, so I put it all firmly out of my mind.

Or rather, I did the best I could. A year or two later, in unrequited love with my best friend and trying to decide what "counted" as being in love, I remember writing something like this in my notebook:

> Am I gay? I know I'm in love with Z. But does that mean
> I'm a lesbian? I'm really too young to decide something
> like that! When I'm maybe twenty, if I still feel like this
> about girls, then I'll decide I really am. But I can't know
> now.

And that's more or less what I did: I waited until college, when nobody I knew was threatening to beat anyone up, and it didn't matter how good anyone was at volleyball, and I didn't feel like my whole world would come tumbling down with one simple "yes."

In the decades since then, most people in my life—my friends and family and even the people I work with have been just fine with who I am and who I love. Even my daughter says that no one at school gives her a hard time about having two moms. I know it's not like that for everyone, and I feel really lucky.

At times I wish I'd had the courage to come out sooner, at least to myself. Sometimes, I wish that when Noelle Johnson asked me that question, I'd said "Yes!," swept her into my arms, and given her a big smooch in front of the whole gym class. It would have made for a much better story, even though I probably would've gotten suspended and beaten up.

And at other times I think I was right and smart to wait until it felt safe for me. Life isn't just a story when you're living it, after all. It's easy for me now, safe in my grownup life, to wonder whether it's worse to get hurt, or worse to live scared that you might get hurt. Some kids who come out as teenagers did and do get hurt, in real and lasting ways, and I escaped most of that.

But you know what's weird? No one ever did actually beat me up, even though they spent much of eighth grade threatening to. I didn't even exactly know what "beaten up" meant, even though I spent most of eighth grade being afraid of it.

I do wish I'd been able, somehow, to not be so scared of something that hadn't even happened to me. And to let myself decide for myself what I felt, and what it meant, and what counted as real.

Left Out

~~~~~~~~~~~~~~~~~~~~~~~

VICTORIA DAVIS

Age eleven at the time

The little girl sat at the edge of the classroom—sensing the excitement but knowing her only form of participation could be observation. Squeals of delight came from the popular corner as white and pink tissue paper flew from the gift boxes wrapped in lots of curly ribbon.

She would get a gift too. But if she squealed she would be ridiculed and hear mimicking of whatever sound she made.

No, life was better for her if she was invisible. Teachers were oblivious or chose to tune out her peer-enforced solitude.

She loved people. She loved to tell jokes and laugh. But right now in this classroom, she was the only joke. What would she do wrong today? Oh, it would be something.

And she'd see these girls at church again on Sunday with their curls, angelic smiles, and stockings, looking like the apples of their moms' eyes. Not saying anything, they would steal glances at one another as she spoke up in Sunday School—what fun they'd have tomorrow teasing her about this lesson!

Yet there was a place she could go with complete acceptance. Her mother and father adored her and enveloped her in their respect, love, and care the moment she came home.

And—in her room at night—she'd open her Bible and read of her Saviour. He was a "Man of Sorrows." Enemies hung on his every word looking for their next point of contention with him. This man—this Jesus—knew what it felt like to be alone, to be made fun of even in church. To be left out and not fit in. He understood. He knew.

And snuggled under her covers beside a small lamp in the darkness, they met in conversation, talked about their day, and became best friends.

Fake Friends on Facebook

~~~~~~~~~~~~~~~~~~~~~

JESSICA ZEILER
Middle School

Sometimes I wonder if the universe put an invisible-only-to-me "Mock Me" sign on my back during my middle school years. I really did have a Kick Me sign on my back, one time.

My family moved from suburban Rhode Island to rural Virginia when I was ten years old. I had gotten picked on here and there in Rhode Island but I still managed to make friends and find my niche. I had hopes of finding the same niche in Virginia but it was not to be—the new kids were into country music, colored jeans, and pretending to date one another. I wore stretch pants, liked Disney and Broadway music, and thought boys were gross. Did I mention I was also the only Jewish person in my grade?

The toughest part of my new school was that it was small and private; some of the kids had been there since kindergarten, and many of us were stuck with each other until we graduated from high school. There were few ways to escape the bullies.

I don't even know if I could catalog every indignity I suffered at the hands of my classmates, but a few incidents really stick out.

One group of girls was lower in the social pecking order, so I could get away with sitting near them—though not *with* them since they mostly ignored me or were mean to me. One day the ring leader, who was a very bossy type, started telling me that I couldn't sit near them, that the space was saved for her imaginary friend. I ignored her at first, then brushed it off, but everyone else started sticking up for this imaginary friend who was going to come and eat lunch with them and needed my seat. I finally gave up and ran out of the lunch room, crying so hard I started to panic and hyperventilate.

Another time, a church group came in and handed out Bibles to everyone, despite the fact that my school was supposed to be non-denominational. I opted not to take one since it was a New Testament Bible. Later, on the playground, everyone was reading their Bibles, and one kid asked me why I didn't have one. I tried to explain that I was Jewish, and he said, "Well that means you're going to Hell." The best part was that a teacher lectured the kid about using bad language, while ignoring the obvious insult to my faith.

One girl was obsessed with talking about me having cooties. Any time I accidentally brushed up against her she would scream, "Oh my God, Jessica gave me cooties!"

One boy called me assorted names that were all variations on the word "prostitute." The worst part was that when I told a teacher, she not only didn't do anything about it, but later claimed to have forgotten I ever told her about it. The second worst thing: the principal promised my mother that the boy would be forced to apologize to me, but he never did. The third worst thing? The kid in question was from a family so very rich and powerful that the school's street was named after them. Anyone connecting the dots?

One day I was reading a book and minding my own business when a really nasty girl took a three-hole punch, emptied out all the little punched paper circles in my hair, and made jokes about how I had dandruff.

What do all these kids have in common, besides making my life a living hell? They all now want to be my friends on Facebook.

Facebook, for those of you who don't know, is a website (www.facebook.com) where you can post a profile of yourself and connect with friends. I made a profile about a year and a half ago, and it has been a bizarre social experiment to see all these kids come out of the woodwork. I hadn't seen or spoken to any of them in nearly five years. And to be fair, most switched from picking on me to ignoring my existence by the time we reached ninth grade.

Still, I don't know what instinct makes people seek me out and want to be my fake friend online. Do any of them regret their past actions? Are they curious about what I'm doing with my life, now that I've been out of high school for five years? Or are they just obsessed with having everyone they ever knew in their life as a friend on Facebook?

The funny thing is that during those terrible years, one of my favorite fantasies—besides becoming a famous writer/actress and dating Leonardo DiCaprio—was becoming a famous writer/actress/director who would triumphantly return to my class reunion *with* Leonardo DiCaprio. I would be fabulous and I'd snub everyone who ever hurt my feelings. (Which would probably leave me with about two people to talk to.)

The reality is that I'm not famous, Leonardo DiCaprio still hasn't called me, and I will probably never go to a class reunion. At least maybe not until my tenth year reunion when I have published a Nobel Prize-winning book about my terrible adolescent years, and can really snub my ex-classmates because I'll have exposed their terrible behaviors in an award-winning book.

Or I can try to put it all behind me and just let my old bullies be my fake friends on the Internet, because maybe living well really is the best revenge.

The Pencil Box

~~~~~~~~~~~~~~~~~~~~

SUZANNE MACLYN

Age seven at the time

In second grade, I was the new kid, again. My family moved ten times by the time I was twelve years old. I went to so many different schools that eventually being the new kid became normal for me, but it was never easy. Every time I started a new school, I had no friends, and I didn't know the rules. Sometimes I cried because I did things wrong—or at least the wrong way for each new school.

Going to a new school usually meant that I had learned different things than the kids at my new school. In second grade, I knew how to read and spell better than the kids in my new class. Because of this, my teacher would have me tutor the other kids, most of whom did not speak English at home. We always had a spelling test on Mondays. If kids missed spelling tests because they were absent, she had me give them the make up spelling tests during lunch and recess. That was okay by me since I had no one to play with at recess anyhow. If there were no tests to give, I would pick up all the trash in our classroom. Sometimes I helped the teacher correct papers.

I was only seven years old, but I was tutoring classmates and giving them spelling tests, which in hindsight is just weird. The kids in class sure thought it was, and they were not nice to me at all.

One day I brought a new pencil box to school. I had decorated it by writing "I love Jesus" and drawing special Christian fishes on it. I really liked going to church on Sundays, and thought that my pencil box was pretty. I was sad when the kids in class started to make fun of my pencil box, pointing at it, and singing in a teasing way, "She loves Haysoos!"

Haysoos was a boy in our class, but I didn't really know him. His friend Raul yelled across the class and told me that Haysoos didn't like me. I was angry at the way everyone was laughing at me, and I told him that I didn't like Haysoos either! I finally said that I *hated* Haysoos, even though I had no reason to hate him. Raul pointed at my pencil box and told me that I loved Haysoos. I was confused and told him again that I hated Haysoos. I could not figure out why he kept pointing at me and laughing. Haysoos was mad and he was making mean faces at me.

I wanted to stay in the classroom during lunch, but the teacher needed to lock up the room, so I had to go outside. On the playground, the boys started running around me in circles singing, "You love Haysoos! You love Haysoos!"

I was getting so mad! I didn't even really know Haysoos! Why were they saying this? I screamed at them, telling them I didn't even like Haysoos! When we went back to class, Raul came over to me and showed me the spot on my pencil box where I wrote "I love Jesus."

When Raul read it to me, he said, "You wrote it right here: See? 'I love Haysoos.'"

I argued with him, "That says, 'I love Jesus!'"

Raul retorted, "That *is* Haysoos! Haysoos is spelled J-e-s-u-s!"

Now Raul was trying to give me a spelling lesson. But I still did not understand how J-e-s-u-s could be pronounced "Haysoos," so I just kept fighting with him even though it only made me cry. Finally other students in the class told me that in Spanish, the name "Jesus" is pronounced "Haysoos." I didn't know what to do. I was very surprised, and finally understood why they were making fun of me, but it only made me mad at myself. I felt stupid.

When school finished that day, Raul and some other boys followed me and teased me even more. I was so aggravated that I threw my pencil box into the trash can. I wanted to show them that I did not love Haysoos.

I was very sad when I got home. All I could do was cry when I thought of my pretty decorated pencil box in the trash. I kept thinking of how happy I was when I first brought my pencil box to school, and how sad I was when I found out Haysoos was spelled the same way as Jesus. I was angry that the kids at school were having fun teasing me, too.

I thought that if I threw my pencil box into the trash, Raul and his friends would stop taunting me. Well, they kept harassing me anyway. But I wasn't the only person that they picked on. They were mean to a lot of kids, and even to each other sometimes. I learned to stay away from them whenever I could. Plus I was just waiting. Waiting until my family had to move again. Then I could go to a new school.

CONTRIBUTORS

~~~~~~~~~~~~~~~~~~~~~

SJ Alexander lives in Seattle. When SJ was in school she wanted to be a long-distance commercial trucker or a farmer, but is currently settling for the shame of being a writer.

Kathleen Cecchin is located in Los Angeles via Chicago, where the "Bitch" lived. She is an actor, director, and writer whose work has been seen in films, on television, at Tony-award-winning theatres, and now in print. Her mouth continues to get her into trouble.

Lea Cuniberti-Duran has been living too close to the San Andreas fault (and waiting for the Big One) since 1993. When not running after her three extremely quick boys, she runs her own design studio, lures her husband into never-ending home improvement projects, and dreams of early retirement in a hut by the beach.

Vicki Davis is a teacher, entrepreneur, author, and speaker. She blogs at the Cool Cat Teacher (www.coolcatteacher.blogspot.com), a leading educational blog, and has won many awards for her global collaborative projects. Her compassion for students was profoundly shaped by the four years she spent in elementary and middle school being continually left out and criticized for being different and loving things like computers, in an age when a computer was definitely not cool. Her work has been featured in Thomas Friedman's book The World is Flat, the Wall Street Journal, the Boston Globe, and many other newspapers and media outlets. Vicki lives with her husband and three children in Camilla, Georgia where she loves country living, cooking, and blogging.

elswhere recently moved to Vancouver, Canada with her family. She no longer cares about being popular. Well, not most of the time. She writes the website Travels in Booland at www.elswhere.blogspot.com.

Cindy Emch is a highway poet. She can be found writing reams of valentines and love letters to her adventures on a daily basis. She calls them poems. Her words are salty and crunchy like sweat and gravel, and they tell queer mossy secrets. Cindy's work has been been published in Lodestar Quarterly, There Journal, It's So You: 35 Women on Fashion, Beauty, and Personal Style (edited by Michelle Tea), and numerous chapbooks. She co-hosted The Aunty Cindy and Unka Lynnee Show with Lynn Breedlove on Pirate Cat Radio from 2004 to 2007, and has been a curator for the National Queer Arts Festival since 1995. Emch is the founder and co-host of San Francisco's twice-a-month Queer Open Mic, which features queer folks of all colors, cultures, and creeds performing their awesome lit to encourage the building of bridges between art, community, and revolution

Sarah M. Glover is a recovering C.P.A. who lives and writes in San Francisco. She is currently using her young children as guinea pigs while manically scribbling away about ghosts and fairies. Hopefully, the scribbling will make it into a book before they leave for college.

Tammy Harrison is a wife and a mom to four children. She makes her home in the Hill Country of Texas where even cell phones don't work. Quiet. Peaceful. Serene. Except when one of the kids is screaming. Her website is www.QuiltTherapy.com.

Liz Henry is a blogger, literary critic, poet, translator, and geek. She writes for BlogHer.org, othermag, Metroblogging, ALTA, Composite, and Feministsf.net; and has published poems, translations, and articles in Poetry Flash, Xantippe, Parthenon West, Strange Horizons, other, Two Lines, Cipactli, Lodestar Quarterly, The Encyclopedia of Women in Science Fiction, and Literary Mama. Her website is www.bookmaniac.net.

Lea Hernandez is a twenty-plus-years comics veteran who has published in traditional print and on the web. She is a webcomics pioneer, and one of the first American cartoonists to merge manga aesthetics with illustration and comics art. Her graphic novel series include Texas Steampunk and the tart pop satire Rumble Girls. Lea hated school, made friends with the other weird kids, and tried out for everything. Lea lives in San Antonio, Texas with her husband, two special needs kids, and an ark of pets. Her websites include www.divalea.deviantart.com and divalea.livejournal.com

Amanda Jones was born, raised, and educated in New Zealand, which means, like all New Zealanders, she has a hard time staying in one place for very long. She moved to the San Francisco Bay Area in her early twenties and promptly married an American. In order to have the ultimate cover for her peripatetic nature, she became a travel writer. She now writes for national travel magazines and newspapers. She does this in between raising her two proudly half-Kiwi daughters.

John H. Kim survived fifth grade to go on to a hideous prep school, but then went to a cool college (University of Chicago) and graduate school (Columbia). He moved to California for a post-doc, then fled academia for the programming industry, with writing on the side. He now lives in Redwood City with his wife Liz and son Milo.

Judy McCrary Koeppen lives with her family in the San Francisco Bay Area. She works as a speech language pathologist specializing in early intervention. When not being paid to hang out with really great kids, she chases her own two children and cares for her family's ever-increasing number of pets.

Jason Kovacs is a native of the I-5 corridor whose writing has appeared in Cranky Literary Journal, ZYZZYVA, and Jeopardy Magazine (you could go find all that stuff and read it, except it is all published under Jason's *old* name and Kovacs is his shiny *new* name). Jason does not like cilantro, and does not understand people who do.

Laura (Henry) Kukulski lives in Oakland, California, with her husband, son, and two cats. She paints, makes websites, blogs, and causes mayhem with reckless abandon. Her website is www.laurakeet.com.

Els Kushner is a librarian and writer who lives in the Pacific Northwest with her spouse, their daughter, and far too many books. Her website, Book Book Book, is at www.bookbk.blogspot.com.

Victoria Laraneta is a grandmother of four who visits the small Midwestern town she grew up in every other year (on her way to yet another exciting USC football game). She loves living in the OC with her wonderful husband.

Meredith Lom lives with her husband Andrew and two ferocious eight-pound terriers in a tiny New York City apartment. By day, she is a labor and employment lawyer, but she moonlights as a non-fiction essayist, devoted blogger, and emerging novelist. Her personal website is Meredith's Daily Angst, www.xanga.com/mas88.

Suzanne Maclyn is a wine-tasting, coastal-dog-walking, novice-blog-writing, picture-taking, niece-and-nephew loving, special-event-hosting, meditating, tofu-eating Southern Californian.

Jackie Davis Martin has divided her life into thirds. The first third was spent in the Pittsburgh, Pennsylvania, area (where Kennywood Park is located, still); the second third in New Jersey, where she taught high school and raised two children; and the third third in San Francisco, where she continues to teach, now part-time at City College. Jackie and her husband enjoy—almost relentlessly—the plethora of arts and scenery the city offers. Her names also emerged in those thirds, and, to push the point to its absolute extreme, her birthday is 3-3!

After her short stint as a cool kid, **Katrina N. Mueller** became a pacifist, a doula, a comedian, a loyal member of Table 29, and a non-denominational nerd. She lives in the great state of Washington, although regrettably as far away from Seattle as one can get.

Jennifer Byde Myers has two modes: "Go! Go! Go!" and "Sleep." Raised in Huntington Beach, California, behind the Orange Curtain, Jennifer escaped to U.C. Berkeley for college and has now firmly planted herself in the Bay Area. She spends her days as wife, mother, sister, friend, and daughter while trying to maintain a sense of self, save the world, and make dinner. In between she writes for large corporations and for personal catharsis. She believes Scrabble should always be served with a sparkling wine.

Jackie Olsen writes, and writes, and writes. Her current projects include a memoir about being a feminist stay-at-home mother, and a book of stories with the working title The Neighborhood Stories. She is a photographer and essayist, and is not normally without a good laugh for long. At the moment, she attends one college for library school and teaches at yet another.

Elaine Park lives in Redwood City, California, with her husband, son, and two cats. She loves the Bay Area weather but remains fond of her Canadian homeland.

Michael Procopio lives in San Francisco, but has yet to figure out the precise name of his neighborhood. He is a food blogger who dislikes the word "blogger" almost as much as he does the words "moist," "classy," and "slacks." His likes include the drawings of Edward Gorey, Cotswold cheese, and the musical stylings of Jacques Brel. His websites are www.word-eater.blogspot.com, and www.kqed.org/weblog/food.

Shannon Des Roches Rosa lives tantalizingly close to San Francisco, but doesn't visit nearly often enough (and retrieving her handsome spouse from his workplace does not count). When she is not running herd on her three darling but challenging children, she picks nits out of other writers' works and occasionally even writes herself. She will never surrender her serial commas.

Linda Saslow is a writer in Orange County, California who is married and has two daughters. She is working on a book of short stories. Her website is www.saslowart.blogspot.com.

Jenifer Scharpen lives and works in the San Francisco Bay Area, and is the only one of the six people in her family not currently in school. She reads as much as possible, and takes a whole lot of photographs.

Mary Tsao is a sober, feminist mother who has a nightstand piled high with half-read books. She also is a housewife and a firm believer in the power of group therapy. On occasion she has been known to make money from her writing. Her website is www.marytsao.blogspot.com.

Alison Weiss is a writer and editor living on the coast of Northern California with her husband and two children.

When **Aruni Wijesinghe-Lewis** is neither riding elephants in the hills above Chiang Mai nor communing with the giant stone heads on Easter Island, she is living a quiet life with her husband Jeff and their two cats in southern California. She currently teaches belly dance, shops at Ross, and strives to improve her Spanish by watching La Esclava Isaura on Telemundo. At present she is planning to visit George, the last tortoise of his kind, in the Galapagos. Occasionally, she writes of her misadventures.

Jessica Zeiler lives in Washington, D.C., and would like the world to know that D.C. is not just a city filled with government drones. She enjoys computer games, cooking with curry, and all manners of science fiction. She doesn't write as much as she'd like to. She occasionally takes trapeze lessons and dreams of running away to join the circus.

ACKNOWLEDGMENTS

~~~~~~~~~~~~~~~~~~~~~~

Every person involved in this crazy, whirlwind, bootstrap, less-than-two-months-from-epiphany-to-publication project donated their time and their work. We cannot truly give sufficient thanks for these acts of generosity, but we'll try.

Thank you to the individual authors, who hopefully used their stories to purge past hurts as well as channel triumphs. We promise to sit next to you any time you ask. Please know that your names are written on our notebooks, encircled by inky little hearts that declare us BFF (Best Friends Forever).

Thank you to Lea Hernandez, who sculpted, painted, composed, and photographed our cover art, and whose crackling sense of humor kept us giggling during those last crazy CISWY weeks. *mwah.*

Thank you to book designer Amy Freels, who delurked from the Blogosphere ether, volunteered to create our book cover, and did such an elegant job.

Thank you to web designer Laura (Henry) Kukulski, who invokes such striking designs, and makes them function so intuitively.

Thank you to the proofreaders who signed on despite our boomerang schedule, and who did such thorough and helpful work: Wendryn Barnhart, Mary Beth Gray, Jeanette Hartmann, Meghan Jarzyna, Meg Mikovits, Grace Mitchell, and Katrina N. Mueller. We are grateful that your sharp eyes and Chicago Manuals are on our side.

And a big thank you to Blogger (www.blogger.com) for giving us the perfect online environment (www.canisitwithyou.blogspot.com) in which to launch, discuss, and fine tune our stories before committing them to print.

Shannon wants to thank her husband Craig for all the extra time he let her steal from their family and give to this project, and for having a generous enough sense of humor to float them both. She would like to thank her children for reminding her that there is always time to sing a silly song, and for inspiring this project in the first place.

She would particularly like to thank her mother, Mary Pat Des Roches, and her auntie, Frances Dosen, who spent several days babysitting the three cutest children who ever refused to go to bed so that Shannon could beat on the manuscript.

She would like to thank her father, Gary Des Roches, for being such a wonderful social role model: everyone knew they were always welcome to sit with him. She wishes he could have been here to see her and Jen pull this project off, because she thinks he would have approved of their business model.

She would also like to thank Sandy Fields for providing a quiet, nurturing space for editing, revising, and proofreading.

And a final bottomless thank you to Jen for not telling Shan that this project was crazily impossible, but instead reverting to the vernacular of their shared SoCal heritage with a heartfelt, "Dude! Totally!"

Jennifer would like to thank her husband Shawn for always trusting that she can juggle sixteen things, and for the support on this project and so many others when she remembers that she has no official juggling certifications. Thank you to the rest of her family too, for raising her to think that just about anything is possible as long as you can read and you work hard. She would also like to extend long overdue thanks to. Jeanne G. Mulligan and Mary Eiswerth, two teachers who always thought the best of her. And still more thanks to her children who remind her constantly to rise to the occasion.

She is also deeply grateful to Shannon for including her in various and sundry whimsy including this amazing project, which has been a source of great joy. She can't wait to say, "Most certainly. I would love to participate!" the next time.

All material contained herein © 2007 the individual authors and artists.

Can I Sit With You?

www.canisitwithyou.org

www.ingramcontent.com/pod-product-compliance
Lightning Source LLC
LaVergne TN
LVHW051126080426
835510LV00018B/2260